Default to Bold

Default to Bold

Anatomy of a Turnaround

Rupert Scofield

Introduction

How to get the life you want and leave nothing on the table when you go.

We are all influenced by our parents, and for even the most self-aware, probably more than we will ever know. For some, this means our lives are a never-ending quest to gain approval, even from those who have already passed on to the spirit world. For others, like myself, it means avoiding the mistakes our parents made, which resulted in a life that never realized its true potential for fulfillment and happiness—what Thoreau chillingly called "a life of quiet desperation" where people "go to the grave with the song still in them."

As the title of this book implies, I believe the way to avoid this is to take the scarier, riskier road, over and over again. Whether in business, sport, or life, this is the more certain way to triumph, not the intuitive strategy of playing it safe. How many times have we seen a team get ahead by a few points and then start to play conservatively, only to have their adversary overtake them in the final minutes? (Super Bowl 2018) Or a company that keeps doing what it used to do in the past, because it worked so well, only to discover too late that it has suddenly become irrelevant and is going out of business? (Kodak) This describes the world we live in today, where disruption is the rule rather than the exception.

I write this as the CEO of a global microfinance company that was once number one in every market we entered and is today a billion-dollar social enterprise which, despite great success over the past thirty-three years, finds itself fighting for its very existence. As the aphorism goes, "what got us here won't get us there in the future". But some strategies, like "when in doubt, default to bold", have served us well over time, and have, if anything, grown more relevant as the microfinance industry has grown more competitive.

This book is in some ways a sequel to *The Social Entrepreneur's Handbook: How to Start, Build, and Run a Business That Improves the World*. As with SEH, my goal is to inspire the next generation of leaders, be they young, mid-career ("cross over") or retirees with much business and life experience to offer, looking for a way to "give back".

But this book also may turn out to be a chronicle of FINCA's demise. Yesterday, in a rented conference room at the Schiphol airport in Holland, my shareholders circled me like wolves around a crippled stag, watching for an opening. As I looked at those scowling faces from Holland, Switzerland, Germany, Belgium and Pakistan, representatives of my six institutional investors, I recalled the heady enthusiasm with which we launched FINCA Microfinance Holdings, Inc., in 2011, during happier times both for FINCA and the microfinance industry. Initially, both our social impact and profits were strong, but as competition grew in all our markets and predatory consumer lenders, retailors, mobile phone companies, Fintechs and even utility companies invaded our space, our financial performance began to lag. In the first half of 2014, we lost money for the first time. This was a rude awakening, causing us to focus more on the financial component, versus social, of our double bottom line. Initially, this shift in focus worked: in the second half of 2014 we made our way back to profitability, managing a net income for the year end of $5 million. This was way below our projection of $20 million in the annual plan, but still a move in the right direction.

Then, on February 21, 2015, disaster struck. In Azerbaijan, where we had our most profitable subsidiary and over a quarter of our global loan portfolio, the government announced a surprise 35% devaluation of the Manat against the dollar. This immediately wiped out a third of our $50 million in equity and sent default rates on our dollar loans to our customers skyrocketing as they suddenly owed us a third more in the local currency. FINCA Azerbaijan went from earning a million dollars a month to making a loss of $1 million.

Not everyone was taken by surprise. Connected members of the elite, acting on insider information, made currency trades ahead of the devaluation, making an overnight profit of $64 million.

But our problems were not limited to Azerbaijan. Elsewhere in Eurasia, the impact of sanctions on Russia for Putin's invasion of Crimea resulted in the expulsion of millions of migrant workers from neighboring countries where we had financial institutions: Tajikistan, Armenia, Kyrgyzstan and Georgia. Deprived of this remittance income, the economies of these countries also tanked. Eurasia, once the profit engine of our network, went into reverse, spurting red ink.

Has my strategy of "defaulting to bold" lost its mojo? Are FINCA and I finally going to pay the price for blithely investing in some of the world's most unstable, poorly governed and most physically dangerous countries, including Afghanistan, Pakistan, Haiti and the Congo? At the time, it seemed like a bold but clever thing to do: go to countries currently in the midst of civil unrest and even civil war, where there would be no competition, and then reap the benefits of being "first movers" when peace broke out. Our shareholders, ostensibly all seasoned investors in emerging markets, seemed to endorse this approach. But that was during good times. Now, with our losses mounting, talk of "the mission" and investing in the "fragile states" has disappeared, replaced by icy, recriminating stares. I thought they would understand these losses are driven by events beyond our control. Wrong.

How will this end?

By the time I complete this manuscript—and possibly well before—my fate and that of FINCA will be known. I was wounded yesterday, humiliated and outraged by this group of people half my age trying to take from me this great, billion-dollar global company that took us thirty-two years to build. There is nothing worse than being asked to leave the room while others deliberate over what to do with your company. And you. Why don't they trust me? I have come through so many other crises over the past three decades, and always manage to come out on top. But I am not thirty-two anymore; I am sixty-six. I had hip surgery last spring, and the ankle I sprained on a lacrosse field at Hofstra College forty-six years ago has given me a pronounced limp.

But I'm not done yet. "Other people love to win," a team-mate once said. "Rupert hates to lose."

A voice in my ear whispers: When in doubt, default to bold.

Lesson Learned Swag Box No. 1: The Party's Over

The Azerbaijan-Eurasia experience revealed risks that neither FINCA nor any of our investors or lenders realized existed. The first was the risk of running a financial institution in an oil-dependent country at a time of extreme price volatility. Between April 2014 and April 2015, the price of oil dropped from $110 per barrel to $50 per barrel, as a result of the Saudi strategy of ramping up production to kill off the fracking industry. After a brief period of trying to prop up their currencies, all the governments in the region, led by Russia, let their currencies float. Everyone who was able immediately bought dollars, resulting in a disappearance of local currency in the local banking systems. But no one wanted to take dollar loans, fearing another surprise devaluation, which would have left them owing even more in their national currency. This highlighted the second big unrealized risk, which could be called "Autocrat Risk". All the countries in Eurasia,

with the exception of Georgia, are run by autocrats who care nothing for the people and run the economies for the sole benefit of their families and cronies. In Azerbaijan, the government took measures in addition to the surprise devaluations, like imposing interest rate caps on loans and encouraging borrowers to "negotiate" lower repayments with their banks, that essentially destroyed the micro-finance industry and indeed the entire financial sector. They did this to curry favor with the general public and to avoid sacrifices of their own.

How did we miss these risks? For two decades, we and our investors and creditors had enjoyed an uninterrupted run of good profits. Even as we all recognized our concentration risk, none wanted the party to end.

PART I—DOUBLE TROUBLE FOR RUPERT

It's a warm spring morning in April, 2015, in Washington D.C., and I am out on my deck, sipping coffee, when Mercutio calls. "Hey, dude. How was Istanbul?"

"It was good. Everybody missed you."

Mercutio was in Istanbul at FINCA's global management meeting, which I couldn't attend, as I was still recovering from hip surgery. Mercutio is one of the four Founding Fathers of FINCA and had been our first CEO, handing the title off to me in 1994 and thereafter remaining a very active board member. Mercutio worked for twenty years at the premier restructuring firm Alvarez & Marsal, rescuing big companies from bankruptcy and earning himself huge success fees in the process. He retired at fifty and lives in a $20-million house on a golf course in Scottsdale, Arizona.

I have a feeling he's not calling to tell me how much everyone misses me.

"Afraid I'm going to have to ruin your weekend, pardner."

"What's going on?"

"It's a conversation I had with Iago, as I was leaving the hotel for the airport. He said: 'Mercutio, we need to talk about *regime change*.' I had forgotten about it, but then yesterday I got an email from Benvolio, saying he needs to talk to me. Has he talked to you since we got back?"

"No." My paranoia is zinging off the charts, like a convicted felon's polygraph.

"What do you suppose that means?"

"It means that Iago has peeled off Benvolio."

Benvolio joined the FINCA board about ten years after Mercutio. We go back even further than Mercutio and I, to the lacrosse playing fields at Brown. We called him "Cro", as in Cro Magnon, for his caveman-like build and low center of gravity. After Brown, Benvolio went to Georgetown Law and then joined a law firm specializing in telecommunications. It was good timing, as the mobile phone explosion was just beginning. He gave up law when one of his clients hired him to run their tower company. He's built and sold four companies since then, becoming very wealthy in the process. We've been through many ups and downs during our forty decades of friendship, including our divorces. We almost lost Benvolio to a heart attack several years ago.

"There has to be another explanation," Mercutio insists.

"What other explanation could there be?"

"Maybe he wants to warn us not to trust Iago and Lady Macbeth."

"If that were the case, wouldn't he confide in me first?"

Mercutio is silent a moment. "Good point."

When Iago joined the board of our holding company in 2011, I recognized him instantly as a "political animal". Iago worked at International Finance Corporation (IFC) of the World Bank for many years, after which he became president & CEO of Financierings-Maaatschappij voor Ontwikkelingslanden (FMO), the Dutch Sovereign Development Bank. Rising to the top of these big, international financial institutions requires intelligence, competence and, more than anything else, political acumen.

Lady Macbeth is the board member appointed by International Finance Corporation (IFC) of the World Bank. She is the only female member of our board. We initially bonded, sharing stories of growing up on Long Island and New Jersey in the '60s. But since our performance has deteriorated, I have the impression Lady Macbeth has been enrolled by Iago into his "regime change" agenda. Lady Macbeth is a tough cookie. A woman doesn't rise to become General Counsel of IFC if she crumbles under pressure in that misogynistic world. I think it's not so much that she wants me gone as she is excited about promoting my COO, Rosalind, into my place. It's a girl's club thing. Lady Macbeth's saving grace is that after three or four glasses of Sauvignon Blanc, what was top of mind becomes tip of tongue.

As he predicted, Mercutio's news spoils my weekend.

My jihad to survive as CEO of FINCA Microfinance Holdings has begun.

A DRESSING DOWN

A week later, I trot over to Pennsylvania Avenue for a meeting with Edmund, our investment officer at IFC. Edmund and I bonded during a snowy evening in the UK on an unheated bus taking us from Cardiff, Wales to Heathrow Airport, which had been closed by a snowstorm. I awoke in London the next morning with what felt like a knife in my chest. A trip to the doctor confirmed that the ride in the frigid bus had resulted in pneumonia.

Like all our other investors, Edmund seems to have turned into a werewolf since we started losing money.

"We are viewing FINCA as a crisis, Rupert! You must close all of your loss-making subsidiaries. You need to cut 50% of your staff at HQ. Don't delegate this. You must do this personally, to restore our confidence in your leadership!"

Cut staff. Close subsidiaries. The cookie-cutter solution posed by every investor since the dawn of time for a company that is losing money. I explain to Edmund that every single FINCA subsidiary at one time or another was losing money. If we closed them each time they went into the red, FINCA would have disappeared long ago. IFC is supposed to be a "patient, social investor" who understands this.

As for cutting half my staff:

"Edmund, it's taken me three decades to build this management team. If I fire them, we won't perform."

"FINCA has the most expensive cost structure in the industry. Either you make drastic reductions, or I won't make any further investment."

He has a point on the costs. I have always tried to hire the best talent, and invest in the best technology, and this costs money. By now, we were supposed to have the scale and revenue to support this, but the crisis derailed all that. I have to own that there have been fuck-ups as well, like Ecuador, where we hired a disastrous CEO who nearly destroyed the bank. But given time, I know we can turn this around.

Edmund has other news for me. He is being promoted and sent to India. I congratulate him, thinking this could be good news for me. I am about to learn that with IFC, you can always do worse.

Edmund takes me down the hall to meet my new investment officer, Oswald, a South American. Oswald has been with IFC his entire career, over thirty years. I try to speak to him in Spanish, to establish some rapport, but he's having none of it. He takes my business card, scans it into his IPhone, and hands it back.

"I have a feeling we will be talking a lot," he tells me. His demeanor turns less menacing. "We like FINCA for the social impact you are having, Rupert. But you have to also make money. They tell me you are a nice guy, but this situation calls for some very hard decisions."

I endure the supercilious dressing down, knowing that until we get back into the black, I have no choice but to put up with it. I hate being in this position. I know Oswald's characterizing me as "a nice guy" is a euphemism for being weak. In fact, I have downsized staff twice during my tenure, the first time by 30% when George W. Bush took us to war in Iraq and all our USAID funding dried up overnight. It's pointless to argue with him. When these "false narratives" take hold in an institution, they are impossible to change.

Lesson Learned Swag Box No. 2: When the Shit Hits the Fan, Secure the Fan
If the reader gleans but one useful lesson from this book, let it be this: If you are the founder of your company,

**NEVER LOSE CONTROL. This means retaining major-
ity ownership over the company, and keeping a majority
on the board of directors. Forget all the "Best Practice"
bullshit they feed you in business school about recruiting
independent board members and rotating off long-time
board members. Recruit your friends and long-time con-
fidants. They need to be competent, but they also need to
be trustworthy. People you've known and worked with
all your life, and have passed the litmus test of absolute
loyalty. People who, when the crisis hits and your shareholders and outside board members turn on you, you can
absolutely count on to vote with you. If I have survived
at the end of this drama, it will be because we somehow
managed to stay in control.**

July brings hot, humid weather to Washington and more
bad news from Azerbaijan. To curry favor with our customers,
who have still not recovered from the devastating impact of the
February devaluation, the government mandates an interest rate
cap on all microfinance loans, well below what we need to break
even. Our losses in Azerbaijan increase from $1 to $2 million
a month. Despite Oswald's threat to speak with me often, the
summer passes with no calls from IFC. All the International
Financial Institutions have generous leave policies, and I assume
my new tormentor is on extended summer holiday. At FINCA,
we cancel all leave and spend our summer toiling away in preparation for a shareholder call in September. We look forward to
this encounter with the relish of a seventeenth-century heretic
anticipating his interview with the Spanish Inquisition.

September arrives and still nothing from Oswald. A sixth
sense tells me something is amiss. Our quarterly shareholder
call is just two weeks away. I take the initiative and make an
appointment to see him.

Not that I expected him to, but Oswald doesn't look happy
to see me.

"What did you want to talk about, Rupert?"

I give him the latest update on our performance. We lost money for the first six months, but July and August were positive. If we can keep this up, maybe we can end the year with a small profit, as we did in 2014. I take it as evidence we are turning things around. I can see Oswald isn't really listening.

"What I really want to talk about, Oswald, is IFC's behavior."

Now he's paying attention. "What do you mean?"

"Your people in the field are telling my people they have orders not to work with FINCA. In Afghanistan, IFC blocked a loan guarantee that would have avoided a million dollars in foreign exchange losses. In the Congo, IFC is holding up a technical assistance grant to help us build out our agent network. What's going on, Oswald? This is really hurting us and slowing down the turnaround."

"Oh, Rupert, this is nothing compared to how we could hurt you!"

I can't believe this. Our anchor investor, threatening to destroy us? But he isn't finished.

"I'm afraid I've got bad news, Rupert. We have taken the decision to replace you with a Restructuring CEO. We gave you your chance, but since we last spoke you haven't fired a single employee or closed any of your unprofitable subsidiaries. You don't seem to feel any sense of urgency."

Sense of urgency. I would hear that phrase a lot over the next several months. I try to remain calm, but my heart is pounding. "And who is this Restructuring CEO?"

Oswald demurs. "We have not yet identified the person. We are undertaking a search."

So there is still a chance I can head this off. I need to go on the offensive. Default to bold.

"Oswald, you don't know FINCA as I do. You have not visited us once, even though we are just down the street. You're relying on someone else's assessment of the situation. Who is advising you to do this?"

"People who are very close to FINCA," Oswald replies, evasively.

"You're getting bad information, Oswald. My years as a consultant taught me when you get the analysis wrong, you make bad decisions." Now I'm lecturing Oswald. I can see it's going over really well. "If we take such drastic action, I promise you, IFC is going to lose a lot of money."

A trace of doubt crosses Oswald's face. There is nothing an international bureaucrat fears more than being tagged with big losses. No one wants to be responsible for having taken a decision that creates an even larger problem than the one he is trying to solve. That is why decision-making in these big bureaucracies is glacial. Everyone hopes to be gone, on another assignment, when the fruits of their bad decisions go rotten.

Oswald picks up his landline.

"Pauline? Come to my office, please." Oswald looks thought-ful. "We better get my staff and your staff together. But we need to do this immediately. Decisions must be made!"

On the ten-block walk from IFC on Pennsylvania Avenue back to FINCA's HQ on 15th and Main Street, I call my wife, Lorraine. I hate to worry her—she's had a terrible year, hav-ing lost her mother in the spring—but she won't want me to keep this to myself.

"I just got fired."

"What! By whom?"

"IFC."

There is a pause. "You don't work for IFC."

"True, but they seem to think they can change me out."

"Don't you control the board?"

"We do, but it's not that simple. Our shareholders in the holding company are the same institutions who have lent us over $800 million in loans. They can put huge pressure on us if we don't to do their bidding."

The line is silent. "Come home. Let's talk about it."

Lesson Learned Swag Box No. 3: You're Not the Boss of Me

Back in the '70s and '80s, When I worked in the Labor Movement, a crusty old telephone worker named Al Moore gave me advice on how to deal with the U.S. Embassy and with USAID, who funded us. "Get along with the Embassy, Rupert, but not too well. Get along with USAID, but not too well. They will treat you like you're one of their employees, if you let them. Don't let them."

IFC is a big, powerful financial institution. But Lorraine was right: I didn't work for them, I worked for FINCA. The same goes for the rest of our investors. When everything is going well, they treat you like a partner. The minute things go wrong, you become their employee whom they are free to sack. Don't let them bully you. Default to bold.

CEO, RESTRUCTURE THYSELF

We live in Bethesda, at the end of Massachusetts Avenue, in a neighborhood some real estate developer christened with the pretentious sobriquet "Glen Echo Heights". Architecturally, it was an eclectic community when we moved there twenty-one years ago, but lately all the '60s, '70s and circa-'80s dwellings are being demolished to make way for six-bedroom McMansions that would look more at home on five-acre plots in Potomac than on the ¾-acre footprints available in our neighborhood. Our kids have moved out and we should downsize, but at the end of the day's travails I love to stand on the rear deck with a drink in my hand, watching the sun set and reviewing the day's triumphs and catastrophes.

From my deck I can see across the Potomac to Fairfax, Virginia, some ten miles distant. As the setting sun paints a rust-colored band across the western horizon, I reflect upon how, just three years ago, I was on top of the world. I had realized my life-long dream of publishing a book, FINCA was profitable, and I seemed to be gliding towards a comfortable semi-retirement where I would hand off operational responsibility to my successor, Rosalind, while I flew around the world making speeches and closing the occasional major deal. Now, suddenly, I can take nothing for granted. The problem of FINCA's survival has been re-dimensioned to the more immediate question of my own survival.

In the warm embrace of a double Knob Creek, I get an idea. Oswald wants to replace me with a Restructuring CEO. What if we restructure the holding company ourselves? No one knows more about restructuring than Mercutio. I will ask him to create a Restructuring Group (RG) to seize the march on Oswald. Further, I will ask our new board member, Prince Hal, who has been appointed by our German partner, Kreditanstalt Fur Wiederaufbau (KFW), if he will also serve on it.

I met Prince Hal in Frankfurt and I think we hit it off. He has an unusual backstory for someone working at an international financial institution. He served in the German army for several years before making a career U-turn, joining KFW and getting into international development. He tells me the decision point came when one of his comrades stepped on a mine in Kosovo. His friend was severely injured and Prince Hal got hit with some of the shrapnel. Prince Hal will add the balance to the RG so that it doesn't appear an all-FINCA entity. More important, he will ensure that neither Iago nor Lady Macbeth are on it.

Lesson Learned Swag Box No. 4: The Wisdom of Al Capone

I genuinely like Iago and Lady Macbeth, and am convinced they probably like me. But don't confuse this kind of "like" with the affection and loyalty your long-time friends feel for you. These newcomers are developing their own prescriptions for how to "save" FINCA, based on their experience with similar situations. Their remedies may not involve you—except in the sense of you going away. Even as you maintain your pleasant demeanor towards them, never expect them to behave in a way inconsistent with their ultimate goal of making you disappear. There is only one practical response to this: Make them disappear. As De Niro's Capone put it: "Somebody messes wid me, I'm gonna mess wid him."

I float the idea of an in-house restructuring group at our meeting with IFC, and, to my delight, they accept. KFW's shareholder representative, Cornwall, shows up at the meeting and also approves. With IFC and KFW in agreement, the other minority shareholders will come along.

The relative success of the Washington meeting raises my expectations for the shareholder meeting. Maybe it won't be so bad. At my suggestion, we decide to have an in-person meeting, in Amsterdam, instead of a teleconference. A face-to-face meeting will minimize the risk of misunderstandings and everyone going home with a different (mis)understanding of what was agreed.

Contrary to my expectations, the Amsterdam meeting is a total debacle. The minority shareholders vie to outdo each other in rudeness and hostility. IFC and KFW have apparently forgotten the positive outcome of our previous meeting and instead show solidarity with the single-percentage shareholders. They play a juvenile game of "Good Cop, Bad Cop", except that the Good Cops have all stayed home. Succession planning is number one on their agenda. Iago has encouraged me to share my succession plan with them ahead of my planned announcement at our December meeting. I should have guessed he was walking me into a trap. The shareholders hate my planned handover in January of 2017, after a year of Rosalind and me serving as Co-CEOs. Why don't I resign in December of this year, 2015, they want to know?

In the afternoon, things degenerate further. At one point, Cornwall, the KFW shareholder representative, after hearing that we have been unable to dispose of a single subsidiary, explodes with rage.

"See! These are things that make us lose confidence! It has been a year now, and nothing has happened!"

Once upon a time in Batumi, Georgia, Cornwall and I took a swim in the Black Sea, in what I took to be a bonding experience. I kept a rock from the Black Sea as a souvenir. I wish I had it now.

The meeting ends with an "executive session", where the minority shareholders have a last opportunity to vent with the FMH board in the absence of management. I go out to meet with the rest of my team at the beer garden. The beer and the autumn sunshine have put smiles on their faces.

"Look, he's still alive!" Rosalind laughs.

"For the time being."

"What can I get you?"

"Nothing Dutch."

"That could be difficult in Amsterdam."

"Fuck it, then. A Heineken."

It's a tribal thing, I tell myself. Just business. Still, this mass rejection stings. I'm unaccustomed to pariah status.

That night, I call my younger daughter, Michelle, who lives in London.

"This is really difficult," I tell her, courting sympathy. "I'm used to being the hero."

"It's good for you, Dad. It will make you more humble."

Lesson Learned Swag Box No. 5: Reasonable Doubts
The duplicity exhibited by IFC at the airport rendezvous revealed two things. First, they lack confidence in their own judgment and decision-making. Second, they are afraid of us for some reason and need the other minority shareholders to do their dirty work. This knowledge will shape our future strategy and tactics.

TROUBLE ON THE CASPIAN SEA

There was a time when I didn't know Azerbaijan was a country, let alone where it is located. The first time I went there, in 1994, the capital city, Baku, was a dystopian landscape of abandoned Russian oil derricks trudging off like rejects from a *Star Wars* audition into the polluted Caspian Sea. There was only one inhabitable hotel, a Stalinist beach resort on the outskirts of the city. Today, after two decades of soaring oil prices, Baku challenges Dubai for the Most Post-Modern Skyline. Over the years, our team did a brilliant job building a large financial institution that was both profitable and delivered significant social impact, reaching at its peak over 150,000 low-income families throughout the country. It was a poster child for how a social enterprise could provide both solid financial performance and social impact. But what goes up must come down, and when the Saudis decided to open the spigots and kill the fracking industry in the U.S., the 60% drop in the price of oil turned our cash cow into beef jerky.

In the midst of this financial tempest, the Restructuring Committee holds its inaugural meeting. Hotspur, FINCA's youngest board member and Mercutio's partner at the work-out firm, is appointed chair. Hotspur tells us he wants to meet telephonically every Tuesday and Thursday for up to two hours a session, until we're out of the crisis. I am reminded of when I was in psychotherapy, back in 1980, trying to figure out what went wrong with my first marriage.

Hotspur was Mercutio's acolyte at Alvarez & Marsal. Hotspur had a unique upbringing. One of his stepfathers was a member of Hell's Angels, which is probably where Hotspur acquired his near-fatal attraction for motorcycles. When he was younger, Hotspur had a close encounter with a pick-up truck running a red light at seventy miles per hour. He wasn't wearing a helmet. After he regained consciousness, five days later, he got right back on his hog. He still rides, today, sans helmet.

"The first thing we have to do is get a handle on our liquidity," Hotspur counsels us. "Once we know our liquidity, my position is that we don't pay anyone. The priority has to be keeping the doors open."

Oh, boy. We have never defaulted, not once, in our thirty-two-year history. If we don't pay our creditors in Azerbaijan, how will they behave in our other twenty-two subsidiaries around the world, where we owe another $500 million (partially to them)? If they all want their money back at once, we will go into a global "standstill", meaning we don't pay anyone. It could end in a great snowball of defaults, rolling downhill. Hotspur and Mercutio seem calm about this. They've been through this a hundred times.

"The important thing is, everyone has the same information, and everyone gets treated equally," Hotspur explains. "Regardless of when their loans fall due. How much debt do we have coming due before the end of the year?"

"Over $100 million," Horatio, our CFO, answers.

"And in the first quarter of 2016."

Horatio says he will have to check, but it's another good slug.

"I thought so. This is why it's so important to manage our liquidity. If we run out of money at any point, it's *adios* FINCA."

"They will all try to strike side deals with you, but you have to resist," Mercutio counsels. "Once they get the impression someone is getting more favorable terms than they are, the whole thing falls apart."

"How many lenders are we talking about?" Hotspur asks.

"Seventeen, just in Azerbaijan. If we're talking global, it's over fifty."

"And we owe how much? Globally?"

"About $800 million."

This last data point is absorbed in silence. I may as well say it before they do.

"You guys tried to warn me. You told me we were borrowing too much money. I didn't listen."

Lesson Learned Swag Box No. 6: We Can Work It Out
If your social enterprise has investors and/or creditors, make sure you recruit someone with experience in restructuring on your board. They don't have to have worked in a restructuring firm, necessarily, as Mercutio and Hotspur have, but they must have been in a position of authority in a firm that went through this process so that they are thoroughly conversant with the process and will not be surprised by how the shareholders and creditors behave. When the storm hits, make sure that your restructuring lead gets out ahead of the shareholders and creditors and steers the process. It is fine, and even desirable, that the creditors form a Lender Group, but don't let them call the shots. If you find yourself in a reactive mode, you will find yourself at their mercy and forced to swallow a lot of very unfavorable terms, some of which could result in your liquidation.

Finally, don't think that because they call themselves "social investors", this means they will be concerned with your survival. On the contrary, at least some of them may use this as a way to disarm you and exact further concessions. Others may have invested in your competition and see an opportunity to remove a player from a crowded field.

The next day I meet at my house with Rosalind and Kate, my deputy, to see if we can come to alignment on our "global footprint" before we meet with the Restructuring Committee. It is not an easy meeting. If I am known for being a dead-ender, fighting to keep every FINCA subsidiary alive, Rosalind is at the other extreme. At the first sign of problems, she wants to sell the sub and bail. She tells me that as a young girl, growing up on a farm in West Virginia, she was assigned responsibility for deciding which of the young chicks got culled before winter came on, as there wasn't room for them all in the chicken coop. My position is that almost any problem can be solved if we have the right management. This is not the case right now in Mexico, El Salvador and Uganda, all of which are programs Rosalind wants to sell or shutter. She says, correctly, that we don't have the capital to feed our entire network of twenty-three subsidiaries. In fact, right now, we don't have any capital, and our shareholders are refusing to invest more, even in our large, profitable subsidiaries, like Pakistan and the Congo. I wonder if they aren't deliberately trying to starve us into bankruptcy. All of them are heavily invested in our competitors, something I didn't pay much attention to when we organized FMH back in 2011. I see now this constitutes an enormous conflict of interest.

Lesson Learned Swag Box No. 7: Curb Your Enthusiasm Partnerships are like marriages, in the sense that the vast majority are entered into with heady enthusiasm and a focus almost exclusively on the upside. In the case of our holding company, despite our protracted, lawyer-led negotiations, which risked breaking down several times over issues like rights of first refusal on exits, tag along and drag along, we still missed some important downsides to what at the time we took to be a near-perfect union and alignment of interests. The big advantage—or so we thought—was that we had been working with these organizations on the debt side for over two decades. We thought they were the right partners for us because they shared our social mission. The big thing we missed is that

they were all invested heavily in our competitors. This meant they had access to all our strategies and investment budgets, and could compare these and determine where they would place their bets and how much. To mitigate this obvious conflict of interest, our investors pointed to the existence of "Chinese Walls" between their debt and equity groups. They assured us these Chinese Walls existed in the heads of their employees, many of whom served as directors for both FINCA and our competitors. In one case, one of our board members was also the chair of a competitor in the same African markets as us. This was not disclosed to us; we heard it from one of our vendors. When confronted with this glaring conflict of interest, our other outside board members defended the arrangement, insisting that "if it were anyone else there might be a conflict, but not with Martin."

When entering into a partnership, Curb Your Enthusiasm and undertake an objective analysis of the areas where your interests may NOT be aligned with those of your potential partners. Also, with the private equity investors and the lenders, look behind them to see who has invested in them. Individuals? Retirement funds? Other funds? Your investors' investors may have different constraints and priorities that kick in during times of trouble, and best to know that before you leap. You may decide to proceed with the partnership anyway, but at least you can be better prepared for the collision when it comes.

The footprint discussion continues into the afternoon. Rosalind says we have to sell Afghanistan as well. Afghanistan? We went there after 9-11, to help rebuild the country, then brought the program back from Death's Door after a huge employee fraud almost wiped us out. Perdita, a former Citibanker who was born in Afghanistan, rebuilt the management and turned it into the number one microfinance company in the country.

"I spoke to Perdita, and she's really worried about the security situation," Rosalind tells me. "She thinks we could lose a million dollars next year, if things don't improve. That will mean we get cut off by our lenders. She thinks we should sell out or find a merger partner."

Perdita is one of the bravest women I know. She took the CEO job at FINCA Afghanistan when there were few men I know who would do that. If she's worried about the security situation, then I'm worried. I tell Rosalind I want to postpone the Afghanistan decision until I talk to Perdita, in early December, when I will go to Pakistan and Kabul.

"We've got to get the footprint down to no more than a dozen," Rosalind reminds me.

"Who says? IFC?"

I know I'm not helping myself. I'm playing into the narrative that *Rupert can't bring himself to part with any of his "children"*. It's not true, is it? I have been trying my damnedest to find a buyer for Ecuador, which is our second biggest crisis after Azerbaijan. Ecuador used to be our best performing subsidiary, but was destroyed by a series of weak managers. Recently, the Supervisor has told us that if we continue to make losses, he is going to intervene us. He suggests we find someone to buy the bank. We have one indicative offer, from an NGO called Fundacion Alternativa, run by a guy named Freddie who moves at the pace of a Galapagos Giant Tortoise with ankle weights. There is a method to his plodding gait. Freddie knows that each day that passes, we lose more money and the price goes lower. Seems like everyone is waiting for us to fail so they can pick the meat off our bones. Recently, two other bidders have entered the competition, which I hope will light a fire under Freddie, *La Tortuga Gigante*.

The next day brings three pieces of news, two bad, one good. The bad news, which Iago brings back from Amsterdam, is that the shareholders are preparing a letter for us. "And while I have not actually seen it, I have been told the contents will deliver a tough message for the current management."

The second piece of bad news is that one of our potential buyers in Ecuador, a large credit union, has dropped out. Their CEO, with whom we had been negotiating, has been sacked by his board. The financial sector of Ecuador is sliding into chaos. Since the price of oil dropped, over $2 billion in savings has run out of the country. Liquidity is tight; no one is lending. Banks are laying off staff.

The good news, sort of, is I have a potential buyer for our sub in El Salvador. I met Gustavo, president of Optima Finance, at a conference in Amsterdam sponsored by one of our investors, Triodos Bank. Gustavo has an MBA from Harvard and worked on Wall Street several years before deciding to go back to his native country and use his skills to help with the situation there.

"When I first got back here, I thought: 'Wow! What have I got myself into?' Gangs, corruption, murders, drugs—what a disaster El Salvador had become. But when I started working, I thought: 'It's not so bad, and I'm doing something important here, much more powerful than just making money for rich people on Wall Street.'"

Gustavo, although he has never said as much, probably belongs to one of the "Fourteen Families" of El Salvador who own most of the businesses in the country. They used to own all the farmland too, until the Land Reform I worked on back in the '80s took it away from them. Gustavo doesn't seem to harbor any ill will. "The country needed to change," he tells me.

Over several scotches, steaks and a bottle of Napa Cab, Gustavo and I shake hands on a deal. Rupert has sold the first of his "children".

Lesson Learned Swag Box No. 8: A Whole New World
I find I am encountering more and more Gustavos around the world: bright young men and women from wealthy families in Latin America, Africa and Asia who study and work abroad a few years and then return home

to build businesses there, creating jobs and trying to put a dent in poverty. It fills me with hope: if enough young people who have lived in a society with rule of law and a more or less functioning justice system repatriate and occupy positions of influence, maybe developing countries will become more progressive. We need to encourage and support these young entrepreneurs. They are building the New World.

SHARPER THAN A
SERPENT'S TOOTH

Iago sends a message through my EA, Isabel, that he wants a face-to-face meeting. He's my friend again, offering to write a letter to the shareholders, entreating them to reconsider their decision to block the appointment of our candidate for independent board member. Our candidate has a great background in financial technology, expertise totally lacking on the FMH board at present.

We undertook this search at their request. The process took a full year. First, Iago and Lady Macbeth each came up with shills known personally to them, which the FINCA board members rejected as an obvious attempt to tip the balance of power. Now the shareholders are refusing to approve what they said they wanted: a truly independent board member with ties to none of the existing investors. Why are they blocking her, then?

"It's the only thing they control," Iago explains. "They need a way to voice their displeasure."

That most lofty of human emotions: spite.

"I will write them two paragraphs reminding them of all the work we put in to screen these candidates, and that if we have to start all over, it will take a long time. I will also tell them that we need to think of the future, even as we struggle with the problems of the present."

Go for it, Big Guy.

Hotspur calls to tell me he is drafting an email to the shareholders, telling them to leave management the fuck alone so we can focus on the turnaround. I'm feeling supported by the entire FMH board for the first time in months. I'm going to need it. Wait until the minority shareholders hear we lost $3 million in September. A second half turnaround, which saved us in 2014, is looking increasingly unlikely. Azerbaijan is just too big, and its losses are dragging us down. I've been holding off, awaiting confirmation from Finance, who has been scrubbing the numbers. Sometimes it turns out that the subs have made errors, and it's either worse or better than the first cut. Please let it not be a swing to the dark side.

The shareholder letter Iago warned of arrives. It's even worse than expected. Iago's mission to save our board candidate has failed. The shareholders say they are "not ready to approve her" and will make a decision after the December 17 meeting. By then, if our candidate has a brain in her skull, she will have figured out FMH is a dysfunctional mess and she would be better off auditioning to play first clarinet for the Titanic Philharmonic. Furthermore, while they "deeply appreciate the services of Rupert Scofield since FINCA's inception", they want me to resign as CEO and put Rosalind in charge effective January 1, 2016. They certainly have made me feel "deeply appreciated" these past months. As to my resignation, they can, with my own "deep appreciation", stuff it.

In a way, this letter is a Godsend. By stalling on our candidate, they punch Iago in the face, and by rejecting our succession plan, they basically tell the whole board, Iago and Lady Macbeth included, to fuck off. Total war! I love it.

Best of all, because we added Hotspur to the FMH board in anticipation of the addition of an independent member, we now have a board with five FINCA people on it, increasing our majority!

But the week is not done with me. Just when I think things could not be worse, my VP of Social Enterprise, Autolycus, drops a second torpedo on my head. Autolycus has been at FINCA for a year and half. I hired him to help me start up a new line of business in non-financial services at the foundation after he was downsized at Deutsche Bank. Autolycus is something of a hero to us in the microfinance industry because he was catalytic in putting together the Microfinance CEO Working Group (MCWG), a coalition of the pioneer networks like FINCA, Grameen, Opportunity and ACCION, created to address industry issues like client protection. His first year with FINCA, Autolycus hired a small army of interns, mostly newly minted MBAs from Johns Hopkins, Georgetown and George Washington University, who researched over a hundred social enterprises working in the healthcare, education, water-and-sanitation and renewable energy spaces. He identified dozens of startups that had developed products, like solar lanterns, that were having a transformative impact on the standard of living of people subsisting on a few dollars a day, literally moving them from darkness to light. It was looking like the initiative we had christened "FINCA Plus" could become as revolutionary as microfinance was thirty years ago.

Lately, Autolycus has been behaving strangely, not coming to the office and failing to return my phone calls.

"Rupert, I have taken the decision to leave FINCA."

It is not good practice to fire people on the phone. Here is Autolycus, quitting on the phone. I ask him why.

"You don't pay me enough, Rupert. I can't afford to keep my kids in private schools. I know FINCA is having financial problems right now. Plus, I want to be a CEO."

I want to say, "Hey, good for you, man. My kids went to public schools." Instead:

"But what will you do, Autolycus?"

He breaks vague here. Mentions setting up an investment company with money from some investors he worked with at DB. Keeps saying "I want to be totally transparent with you, Rupert."

Sproing!

My Spidey Antennae pop up from their small pouches behind my ears.

Lesson Learned Swag Box No. 9: Methinks the Lady Doth Protest Too Much

When someone keeps telling you how transparent they are, you can be sure they are hiding something from you. Watch your back.

Lesson Learned Swag Box No. 10: Heed the Meek, Not Just the Mighty

Tito Castro, an ally-turned-adversary who worked for me when I was working on the land reform in El Salvador in the early '80s, taught me to cultivate people in low places as an important source of intel. When Tito would come to see me at my fortress-cum-office in a toney section of San Salvador, he would always stop first to chat with the people who took care of my daily needs, people who are invisible most of the time, whom we often forget have eyes and ears. Gardeners and guards see who comes and goes to meet with you each day. Drivers are privy to many "classified" conversations that take place as you move from one appointment to another. Maids know who sleeps with whom. Cooks overhear interesting, unguarded conversations when their employers have had one too many.

My own son, John, who was doing a stint in Ecuador as a volunteer credit officer at our bank, warned me that our CEO, desperate to address a huge attrition problem, was sending newly recruited credit officers into the field with less than a week of training. John was in a position to know, but I foolishly ignored his intel. A half year and millions of dollars in losses later, we finally sacked our CEO.

As CEO, pay attention to all the informational channels available to you, especially the informal ones. The person

you least expect may be the source of the information that saves your company. And, if you ignore them, the reason you fail.

Two days later, Autolycus takes me to "Power Africa", an event at the White House to celebrate Obama's solar energy initiative to bring power to millions of off-grid African families. In attendance are representatives of over fifty solar companies from around the world. Autolycus suggests we split up in our networking to cover more ground. I see him in earnest conversation with some of the entrepreneurs, as if he were still hard at work for FINCA, up until his last day.

Sproing!

After the event, Autolycus and I repair to the balcony off my executive conference room to talk about how to handle his departure and transition to whoever will take over. I am still struggling to make sense of this seemingly irrational career move. How is he going to support himself while he's standing up this new company? I'm annoyed he's leaving me in the lurch, without a successor.

"Just what is your company going to invest in?" I ask.

"Well, in all these solar companies."

SPROING!

"The same ones we've been talking to here at FINCA?"

"That's right, Rupert."

I am out of my chair now. "Autolycus, do you realize what you're saying? I paid you to research those companies. That's completely unethical!"

Autolycus looks at me as if he doesn't understand. "Why do you say that?"

"Are you serious? You're a fucking swindler, Autolycus! You've been moonlighting on me the whole time, haven't you? You don't see that that's unethical?"

He shakes his head. "I don't see it that way, Rupert," he insists.

I feel like a cuckolded husband who has just discovered his wife has been sleeping with his neighbor. I gather up my phone and glasses. I rescued him, gave him a job after he got sacked by DB, and this is how he repays me.

"Get out of my company, Autolycus. Before I throw you off this balcony."

A HILL OF BEANS

On November 5, just one week away, my three-year-old grandson, Fordy, has to have a very delicate operation to correct a life-threatening birth defect. The Vein of Galen, a swollen blood vessel in the brain, affects only one child in a million. Ten years ago, most children with this birth defect died before the age of four. Along comes a Mexican neurosurgeon named Berenstein, who invents this incredible procedure where he navigates a catheter the size of a human hair up into the brain and through it injects Crazy Glue into the fistula to seal it off. Fordy has been through this procedure twice before because the vein keeps branching out into new fistulas. Berenstein has agreed to treat him again, and we hope this will be the last time. The previous operation, back in August, was incredibly tricky because one of the fistulas had wrapped itself around Fordy's cerebral cortex.

At the time, I don't appreciate just how great a role neurologists will play in my life.

Compared to this, my problems with FINCA "don't add up to a hill of beans", as Bogey tells Ingrid on the runway in *Casablanca*. In *The Social Entrepreneur's Handbook,* I stated my philosophy that all business problems are good problems, just puzzles to solve. But for the first time since my last *annus horribilis* back in 1994, my first year as FINCA's CEO, when three of our programs exploded at once and I lost a million dollars to a fraud in El Salvador, I am having trouble sleeping. I wake up every night, between 2 and 3 a.m., my worries circling my head like carrion birds over a rotting goat carcass. Normally, a half hour of meditation sends the buzzards flapping off, one by one, and I return to sleep until 6 or 7 a.m. Now a voice visits me each night: "Sleep no more, Rupert! Thy investors hath murdered sleep!"

I know Caesar, our Chairman, will refuse to comply with the shareholders' request to remove me as CEO of FMH, but I also know they will keep the pressure on until they break us. Their next move will be to work the debt side. Ecuador will be the first test. Tomorrow in Santiago, Chile, our CFO, Horatio, will ask three of our lenders to roll their loans over to give us more time to do a transaction. I suspect they may use this leverage to condition their rolling on my stepping down. If they take this action in enough countries, they will destroy FMH. They will also lose not only all their equity but much of their debt as well. Mutually Assured Destruction. They are counting on FINCA to blink first.

They don't know Caesar and Mercutio.

Definitely losing it. Left my laptop at security at Heathrow. "Take this off, take this out, put this shit in the tray, take off your jacket, your belt, your shoes and step into Ming the Merciless's Purple Death Chamber, then 'Reach for the sky, pardner!'" Having a titanium blade in my right leg from my hip replacement means I am always subject to a pat-down, trebling the risk my trays will be usurped by other passengers snatching up their belongings and rushing to make their flights.

Osama grins up at us from his watery grave.

I discover my error when, about two hours into the flight, I decide not to have a second Bloody Mary but do some work. (The Protestant Work Ethic dies hard) Oops. I stare into the empty scabbard muttering fuck, fuck, fuck! No choice but to default to the dusty tools of the past, quill and papyrus. I enjoy the nostalgic ride back to the days before word processors, when I used to write on yellow legal pads and in pencil so that I could write, erase, rewrite, re-erase, re-rewrite, re-re-erase, re-re-rewrite, until I thought it was perfect; or until I had worn the eraser down below the yellow metal band; or until the yellow pad was so scored with erased text that I couldn't read the new stuff, at which point I'd ball it up, toss a three-pointer into the wastebasket, brush the carbon-blackened rubber crumbs off my lap and start on a fresh sheet.

The problem with the tools of the past becomes apparent when I stash the pages I wrote into the seat pocket in front of me, which is where they remain to be discovered by the guy cleaning the plane after we land in Chicago.

Fordy's operation is now just two days away. Maybe it's the approach of the holiday season, or the fact that I'm in O'Hare airport, but I find myself thinking back to 1978, when my first wife, Ginny, was pregnant with Julie, Fordy's Mom. We were stranded in O'Hare airport by a blizzard on our way from Madison, Wisconsin, to St. Louis where we were going to spend Christmas with her parents. Twenty-eight years old and nowhere professionally, I was just another dime-a-dozen grad student making my way toward a master's degree in economics. Ginny's dad considered me a loser, a directionless vagabond who had married above his station, killing time as a student because he had no idea what to do with his life.

The airline naturally wanted us to spend the night in the airport because, you see, they had no control over the weather.

"No, you're going to give us a hotel room."

"Why would I do that, Sir?"

"Because my wife is eight months pregnant and I don't want her sitting in a fucking plastic chair all night."

We got the room at the airport hotel. A month later, Julie was born in Madison, Wisconsin. The next day I went on a six-week consulting assignment in the Dominican Republic, a gig that turned into my first "real job", working for the American Institute for Free Labor Development, a Cold War dinosaur set up by Kennedy and the George Meany of the AFL-CIO to fight communism in the trade union movement in Latin

America. I poured myself into my work for the next three years, travelling my ass off, trying to make up for the late start I got on my career. I was in the Dominican Republic when Ginny called me, in tears, telling me her father had been diagnosed with cancer.

"I need you to come home!" she begged.

I told her I couldn't, I had to finish up my work in the DR. We do stupid things when we are young.

Three years later, Ginny and I were divorced in Washington, D.C.

Lesson Learned Swag Box No. 11: The Vision Thing

People bring conflicting visions into a new marriage, which reflect their parents' marriages. My parents were aloof and uncommunicative; Ginny's were warm and close. I thought I was becoming the kind of husband Ginny wanted, i.e., successful in my career like her dad. In fact, what she really wanted was someone who came home from work every day, and made the young marriage the priority, which was the last thing I offered. I made it worse by totally misreading how to respond to the news that her dad had a terminal illness.

When a family crisis hits and you have to choose between the family and the job, screw the job. Pick the family. If you don't pick the family, you'll regret it. Maybe not tomorrow or the next day, but some day and for the rest of your life. Travel for your work and, if you have any control over it, make sure you limit each trip to no more than two weeks. If you don't, get a new job, or you'll come home one day to an empty house.

GLIMMERS

Finally, a glimmer of good news. Three glimmers, actually. First is that in an edit to Caesar's reply to the shareholders' "nastygram", Prince Hal suggests telling them to fuck off—diplomatically, of course. Our decision on the succession plan will stand; Rupert and Rosalind will be Co-CEOs until 2017. Defense from an unexpected quarter! Benvolio quickly endorses. Iago and Lady Macbeth are silent. Now the count on the board is five to two against the minority shareholders on this issue.

The second piece of good news is that Rocky, our CEO in Ecuador, tells me that we made money in Ecuador this month. Allahu Akbar! Rocky is my go-to guy for all the tough assignments in Latin America, so when Ecuador goes into Intensive Care, he steps forward to engineer the turnaround. Rocky and I go back forty years, to my Peace Corps days when he was CEO of the Guatemalan Credit Union Federation. We were competitors back then, but he came to work for me when I started upgrading my FINCA team—comprised of mostly non-financial people back then—by poaching from the credit union movement. He's been with me for twenty-five years now and is the source of a lot of key intel as to what's going on with the Latin American subs, including who is failing and needs to be changed out. This makes him unpopular, of course, and the non-performers do everything in their power to undermine him.

Lesson Learned Swag Box No. 12: Your Money and Your Life
When you work in the most difficult countries on Earth, it's hard to find reliable, honest and loyal people who will

warn you when things are going wrong and fix them when they do. You need to build, over time, a cadre of people you trust with your money and your life. You also need to understand that loyalty is a two-way street. When a trusted colleague sticks his neck out for you, you have to back them up, especially when their detractors are trying to take them out. No one can do this for you. Relationship-building is not something you can delegate.

Horatio says the preliminary close for October shows us with a loss of "only" $1.2 million, after September's Lollapalooza loss of $3 million. I send off a salvo of emails to the FMH shareholders, containing September's atrocious results and our recovery plan for Azerbaijan. I hear them detonate as they land in Germany, Switzerland, Holland and down the street at IFC.

Meanwhile, down on the equator in Ecuador, it's finally sinking in that in less than a month the Superintendent's Storm Troopers will kick down the front door and take over the management of Banco FINCA. In what has become a grooved ritual, Freddie the Tortuga postpones his offer yet again. Next week, he says. *Mañana.*

I retain my equanimity through all this. Perhaps I am floating down that long African river, Denial. Fighting on so many fronts simultaneously gives me no time to sink into depression and worry about the smaller shit.

I have a rendezvous with Autolycus tomorrow. He's flying in from Dubai today, where he's been shopping the fruits of the research he did while on our payroll. He will be here at FINCA tomorrow, bright and early, looking, as Eric Clapton put it in SWABR, "as if he never, never, never done one wrong thing". I hear murmurings that he is weakening and wants some kind of amicable solution. Fuck that. I want his head on a pike at Traitor's Gate. But I tell my legal team to tell him that all is forgiven, and I just want to talk about transition. Meanwhile, they are to lay a nice ambush for him.

FAMILY MATTERS

Fordy's operation takes place at Mt. Sinai, in New York City, so he has to fly out from Seattle with Julie and her husband Trevor. Julie, like me, is a worrier. Our genes are from a Neanderthal ancestor who lay awake all night at the cave mouth while the rest of the tribe slept, bellies full of mastodon brisket. In the days, weeks and months leading up to these procedures, she becomes increasingly anxious. The day of the surgery starts at 6 a.m. with an MRI and Angiogram to check on the status of the diabolical Vein of Galen.

An urgent call with the board members of the holding to talk about Ecuador serves to distract me from the stress of the waiting room. I walk the streets of the Upper East Side, turning my cell on and off "mute" to drown out the cacophony of the city: trucks blasting up and down the avenues, police and ambulance sirens screaming as they transport people from accident and crime scenes to hospitals and Rikers. New York, New York, it's a hell of a town. A bum in grease-stained clothes staggers towards me, trying to catch my eye, ranting on about someone or something, squaring things with the world as the indifferent *hoi polloi* flow past him on either side, like water around an errant boulder. Ecuador has shouldered aside Azerbaijan as our *numero uno* worry bead. Freddie the Tortuga tells us the most he can pay for our bank in Ecuador is 50% of book, but "it will probably be less due to other risks." This would leave us with insufficient cash to pay off all our lenders. Oh, "and we may decide not to make an offer at all." Meanwhile, two other potential bidders have surfaced. One is a small bank owned by a Norwegian NGO. They are interested "but not in any hurry." The other is someone Rocky met, a guy named Alfonso who has a business selling lie detectors to the government. We met on my last trip to Quito for a whiskey-drenched dinner. He tells me he can read people's handwriting and tell whether they are honest or crooks. He takes a sample from me. "I can see you are an honest man, Rupert," he tells me.

Sproing!

We spend the entire day at the hospital. The operation takes a scary turn, when Dr. Berenstein pierces an artery that was hiding behind the V of G, but he adroitly plugs it with glue and rescues the situation. The problem of the V of G remains unsolved, however, and the way forward uncertain. For now, Berenstein advises we give the arteries in Fordy's head time to mature, after which he may make another attempt. Or the problem may fix itself. It happens.

Not the outcome we'd hoped for. We were desperate for an end to the uncertainty, but it appears we must live with it awhile longer.

Back at the hotel, I know I should go to bed but the siren call of the iPhone seduces me. News of Autolycus. The ambush was successful. A review of the files on his laptop, which my alert HR Director confiscated when he showed up to claim his outstanding travel expenses, reveals documents proving he set up his company way back in July, while he was still on our payroll. They also suggest he corrupted one of our analysts and assigned her to work exclusively on his company.

I suspected Autolycus had Broken Bad, but this is beyond the pale. This is stealing. I take out my Autolycus doll and insert another pin through his forehead.

HAVE I LOST MY WAY OR JUST MY MIND?

When I was a kid, I used to fake being asleep on Sunday mornings to avoid going to church. I've never had religion in the formal sense, but I have a philosophy of life that as long as I am doing good in the world I will be protected from harm. This belief was fortified during the early days of FINCA, when it seemed, after the initial years of struggle, we didn't make a wrong move. Even our most egregious mistakes turned out to be great learning experiences we capitalized on a road that seemed to run steadily upwards.

Lately, I have doubts as to whether FINCA and I are still on The Path. I feel we have strayed somehow and, as a consequence, our protective shield has fallen away. Even our allies question whether FINCA is still relevant in the world, or we've been surpassed by the Second Wave of Innovation. According to this narrative, FINCA was one of the pioneers that opened up the market for microfinance, but now is being "disrupted" by the Digital Revolution. The future belongs to the Fintechs and the mobile phone companies who have millions of subscribers whom they are reaching with financial services by riding the rails of their digital infrastructure. Pretty scary.

The problem with that narrative is that we and the other "Legacy Microfinance Companies" are also embracing the Digital Revolution by partnering with the Fintechs and Mobile Network Operators (MNOs). Unfortunately, we are the weaker, junior partner in these alliances and vulnerable to being taken advantage of. One more thing to worry about.

Meanwhile, evidence that the Boss is losing his marbles mounts. Today, Lorraine and I missed our flight from Johannesburg to Entebbe, Uganda, because my iPhone failed to adjust to Joburg time from our previous location, London. As a consequence, I will miss the inauguration of our new office building in Kampala, which was the entire purpose of my trip. And technology is my friend?

Better late than never. We make a reservation for the following day and check into an airport hotel. Perhaps it's for the best, as we have a fresh crisis brewing in Ecuador and we need to convene an emergency telephonic meeting of the FMH board. Rosalind warns me that since Iago and Lady Macbeth aren't on the Restructuring Committee they have been out of the loop on a lot of things and they are not happy about it. In the past, I always made it a point to keep my board members up to speed on any new developments, but lately things have been moving just too fast to do this. Into this hostile climate I have to introduce a resolution to invest more of our scarce capital in Ecuador. The timing could not be worse. Iago and Lady Macbeth can't block it, because FINCA holds a majority on the board, but they can make it difficult and deliver a flogging in the process.

Iago, Lady Macbeth and Prince Hal listen in silence while I lay out the situation. We have two issues, one dire and one merely urgent. First, we need to put in $500,000 in fresh capital because the monthly losses have pushed us below 50% of our paid-in capital, a violation of the banking regulation and one of the triggers for intervention. But we also need another $3 million during the first quarter of 2016 to meet the new minimum capital requirement, which was raised recently in an effort to shore up the liquidity in the banking system. What I don't tell them is that Rocky, in defiance of Horatio, our CFO, promised the Supervisor that FMH would put in this additional capital. Iago is the first to speak.

"Well, I realize that we are in a crisis, and that we really have no choice, but at some point we need to revisit how we came to be in this position."

"Yes, I agree," Lady Macbeth chimes in. "Can we not just vote to put in $500,000 now, and the rest after we have a chance to discuss this in more detail?"

Like a good former IFC person, Lady Macbeth likes to postpone decisions until there can be more meetings. But it's impossible to convene everyone for another meeting because they're too busy attending meetings.

"I'm sorry," Prince Hal pipes in. "But did we not meet about this just last week? And at that time, Rupert, I do not recall you telling us there was any sense of urgency on this."

I have given up Iago and Lady Macbeth as lost causes, but really hoped to keep Prince Hal on my side. I explain I did not feel any urgency around the capital injection because it is something within our control, whereas the lack of a viable offer to buy the bank remains an imminent threat.

Lesson Learned Swag Box No. 13: All in Favor Say "Aye"
Never put a motion before the board unless you have already made sure that it's going to pass. Enough defeats, and even your allies on the board will begin the search for a new CEO. Do your preparatory work. Speak one-on-one with each board member to assure them you have looked at the problem from all angles, considered all the available options and eliminated them for sound reasons. Don't overcomplicate the decision with uncritical details. Cast the decision in the simplest possible terms, so the board members can see that management's recommendation is not just the best option, but the only option.

Lesson Learned Swag Box No. 14: When in Doubt, Break the Rules

A corollary to Default to Bold is that if you know you are right, don't be deterred by orders from above that don't make sense. Your Prime Directive is to do what is best for the organization, and sometimes the people down in the ranks know better what that is than the High Command. Rocky knew he was safe with me, but he was clever enough not to put me in the position of having to overrule my CFO, which may or may not have worked.

The call concludes quickly after that. I stand alone on the balcony of our hotel room, shortly after midnight, watching the planes land, drinking Johnny Walker Black and reflecting on Iago's words. How *did* we come to be in this position? More important, what could I have done to have prevented it? Why didn't I pay attention to my own son and fly my ass down to Ecuador to investigate? There were other errors too, like allowing Ramon, our star CEO at the time, to postpone building out the savings function in FINCA Ecuador, with the result that we now have to fund 100% of our loan portfolio with debt, grown ever more expensive due to a series of taxes President Correa put on external capital transfers. Our international debt costs us an average of 18%, whereas we can mobilize savings at 6%.

Water under the bridge. Spilled milk. Pick your metaphor. Bottom line: I fucked up. Maybe the shareholders are right to clamor for my head.

MUSEVENI, ME AND IMMORTALITY

Sweet women's voices, singing hymns as FINCA Uganda's driver, Joseph, takes us to Entebbe airport at 4 a.m. on Sunday morning. It was a brief but satisfying stay, despite the embarrassment of missing the inauguration of our new office building. We got to the Sheraton Hotel about 8 p.m. on Thursday night and found Orsino, our Regional Director of Africa, out on the patio with three of his staff.

The Kampala Sheraton has been around as long as FINCA Uganda: twenty-three years. In the early days, while I was still struggling to find funding, I did my business in the lobby of the Sheraton, although I couldn't afford to stay there. Instead, I relied on the kindness of a Swedish World Bank employee whose daughter went to primary school with my daughter back in Washington, D.C. Peder was living alone while waiting for his three daughters to finish school, after which they and his wife would move to Uganda. We did our business during the week, and on the weekends drove down to Entebbe to play golf on a course that was mostly dirt and sunburnt grass, but at $2 greens fees the price was right. On some holes we would find someone's laundry drying on the green, on others someone fast asleep, taking advantage of the flat, soft surface. Fornicating monkeys provided comic relief.

What fun we had back then! Like any start-up we struggled, but microfinance was new and so powerful it was relatively easy to raise money once you got a pilot up and running. Today, we are one of dozens of microfinance banks in Uganda, fighting to hold on to market share. Many of the other banks in the country have surpassed us. It makes me wonder: Are my critics right that FINCA is just good at being the pioneer, bringing the flame to a country, but then unable to scale it and make it profitable? Our strategy was to conquer the world, rather than focus on just a few subsidiaries. Now we are living the downside of that, unable to feed our twenty-three hungry subs and forced to choose among them who gets the worm.

Lesson Learned Swag Box No. 15: The Allure of the New, the Value of the Old

Entrepreneurs have many fine qualities but focus is seldom one of them. We get excited about the Next Big Thing and New Challenges. In my case, it was going to a new part of the world I'd never seen before and starting up a new FINCA program. First it was Latin America, then Africa, then the former Soviet Union countries, and finally the Middle East and Asia. Fine, but someone has to follow in the entrepreneur's wake, making sure the existing infrastructure is taken care of and properly managed. Otherwise you will find yourself, as FINCA has, with Latin America falling behind the competition and creating risks that could bring the whole company crashing down. Worse, now several of our African subsidiaries are showing signs of obsolescence.

It all comes down to management, of course. For the older, more developed markets you need managers who can stay ahead of the competition, either through innovation or simply providing better service. Equally important, your managers need to be empowered to make the required changes, not waiting for permission from HQ or expecting them to come up with the solutions. Above all, in chasing the excitement of the new, don't forget to maintain the value of what you've built.

I spend Friday morning at a FINCA branch a few kilometers outside of Kampala, where I meet with our staff and the members of three of our village banks. I watch our Bright Life team go to work, marketing solar lanterns to the women as they wait for their FINCA loans. The lanterns have a powerful value proposition for the women. The kids can do their homework at night. The lanterns also replace kerosene or paraffin lamps most people use, which saves them $100 a year in fuel (the lamps only cost $50, and, of course, the "fuel" (sunlight) is free) and carries a health benefit in that it eliminates the kerosene fumes. They also prevent tragic accidents, especially during the dry season, when kerosene or paraffin lamps can tip over, igniting deadly fires. Our sales lady demonstrates how these devices also have a socket on the back for charging mobile phones. Eight of the thirteen women buy them; four finance the purchase by topping up their regular FINCA loans by an additional $50.

Bright Life also markets water filters and a clean-burning wood stove that is wildly popular with our women clients. This means that, for less than $150, a poor family can go from darkness to light, from the Stone Age to living like human beings. Our new business line, FINCA Plus, has the potential to be as revolutionary as microfinance was when I practiced it forty years ago in the highlands of Guatemala. I discern a pathway out of the nightmare of angry shareholders and lenders my life has become of late. I will shed my banker's raiment and become an entrepreneur again!

Lesson Learned Swag Box No. 16: Move to the Light
While solving the problems of the present, large and all-consuming as they may seem, keep working on the future. Of one thing you can be certain: your current problems will find solutions, sooner or later, and new problems

will take their place. For your own psychological health, don't allow your adversaries to keep you pinned down to the extent you can't keep the healthy part of the business growing and innovating. If you get caught in that trap, you will find the competition has surpassed you. And your shareholders will be the first to call you out on this, even as they deflect responsibility for having put you in that box.

Now it's time to go to see the bank's new office building, where a board meeting is taking place. The staff is snickering when we arrive. What's the joke? One of them points to the wall above the vestibule, where two medallions have been embedded in the concrete, one of President Museveni and the other of... OMG, they didn't really do that! In jest, I had told the Uganda team that I wanted a statue of Rupert in the vestibule of the new office, standing at the Source of the Nile, holding the hand of a young Ugandan girl and gazing toward the distant horizon, as if at FINCA's brilliant future in Africa.

"Boss, not a good idea," one of my African board members cautioned me. "Too Neo-Colonial."

So they settled on this as a compromise. I have mixed feelings about being outlived by a bronze medallion. Just one more reminder the sands are running out.

BREAKFAST WITH MY ENEMY

The next morning, I have breakfast with Lear, chairman of FINCA Uganda. Lear always has lots of advice for me, particularly these days. Lear had a long, storied career at KFW, the German sovereign development bank, and in retirement he serves on the board of FINCA Uganda. He is also on the board of a microfinance investment fund that finances a dozen of our other subsidiaries. This makes him a valuable ally, but also gives him huge leverage over us at the global level. Too bad I didn't know this when we appointed him. I am generally quite proud of my paranoia, having nurtured it over many years, but this whole experience has taught me to more frequently ask myself: *What are the ways this could all go terribly wrong?*

Lear had some kind throat surgery recently—too many *Habanos?*—which makes him really hard to understand, even in person, and impossible on the phone. It's almost as if he's speaking a glottal Mayan dialect: *opp glop chock mock blop.* Lear tells me that things in Azerbaijan and the rest of Eurasia are not going to get better anytime soon. We need to expect another round of devaluations, which will give rise to another round of defaults in our loan portfolio.

"The rumor in the market is that FINCA is going bankrupt," Lear tells me. "You run the risk of the lenders refusing to renew their loans."

I tell Lear I have heard this same thing from the IFC. I don't tell him that IFC is a principal source of these rumors and was putting out this message even before the catastrophe in Eurasia struck.

"You need to send a strong signal to the market, Rupert. Do something dramatic, like cut out half your costs at headquarters."

Where have I heard this before? I had always considered Lear a friend and ally, but he seems to subscribe to the same cookie-cutter solutions to performance problems as IFC. He's never actually run a financial institution, but thinks he knows how to, which makes him dangerous.

I tell him we are planning a reduction in our footprint, and this will be accompanied by a downsizing in our staff. Lear nods, approvingly.

"Another part of the rumor is around your compensation. You know, Rupert, your salary is posted on the internet. Everyone knows that you make $700,000 a year, during a time when FINCA is losing money. It is creating a lot of outrage, I must say."

"Lear, I do not make $700,000. I used to make $400,000, but since the crisis hit all of us in top management have taken a 10% cut." I explain that the $700,000 number owes to a retirement program the board set up for me, which the IRS taxes as if I had received all the money the year it vested, when I turned sixty-five.

"You should pay yourself zero," Lear advises me, not having heard a word I said. He leans forward, lowering his voice as if sharing a big secret. "You can afford it!"

How has Lear come by such an intimate knowledge of my personal finances? I wonder. "Lear puts people in one of two boxes," Prince Hal, who considers himself a Lear protégé, told me once. "Either the positive box, or the negative box. And once you are in that box, you can never get out."

"And which box am I in?" I asked.

"Lear hates you."

Lear rises to go.

"Wait a minute, Lear, I have a bone to pick with you also." I have decided not to leave the conversation one-sided.

"What is your bone, Rupert?"

"Rosalind and Mike and I think we should change out the CEO. FINCA Uganda is losing market share and the profitability is shrinking. Peter has had three years to turn it around, and he's not performing."

"Peter is performing, in my judgment." I wait for him to add: *And mine is the only thing that counts.*

Now Lear is on his feet. He sticks a finger under my nose.

"And another thing, Rupert. If Peter goes, I go."

Lesson Learned Swag Box No. 17: Do Your Due Diligence

Darwin Eads, the friend I quoted in *The Social Entrepreneur's Handbook*, told me that we spend more time researching the specs of a $500 piece of office equipment than we do a potential employee who may generate millions in revenue if they work out and cost us that or more if they screw up. The same goes for prospective board members. Before you take them on, research all their affiliations thoroughly, and, if they have served on other boards, get references as to how they played in the governance sandbox. Are they dictatorial? Do they insist that everyone follows their advice, right or wrong? You can't be too cautious, as we will see later on in this narrative.

CRY, THE BELOVED COUNTRY

Next stop is Cape Town, where I am attending a conference put on by Mastercard Foundation, one of our major donors, but also redeeming a long-standing pledge I made to Lorraine to take her to New Zealand. Well, yes, we are in South Africa, which is not Kiwi Town but the best I could do given what a manic year it has been.

The next day, at the conference, I speak with the IFC man in charge of Africa. I want to learn the fate of a Technical Assistance grant to build out an agent network in the DR Congo that I was told by Edmund had been approved and was pending disbursement. He shakes his head. "We'd love to work with FINCA, Rupert, but there's nothing I can do until HQ lifts the curse on FINCA."

He suggests I talk to Theobold, a veteran of the microfinance movement and the closest thing I have to an ally at IFC. After the last session, while the conferees are guzzling South African chardonnay, I intercept Theo on his way to the *hors d'oeuvres* table. He suggests we find a table in the back where we can talk in private. I ask him if there is any chance that IFC HQ is going to quit screwing FINCA.

Theo's brow knits with consternation. "Yes, I'm worried about that. I saw an email the other day that said IFC is considering putting FINCA into the 'work out' group. These guys are not like the Risk Group at KFW, who will work in cooperation with operations. They have one goal which is to… to…"

"Liquidate FINCA?"

"Yes, exactly. A number of us are pushing back on that, of course, but you never know how it's going to play out."

Theo has yet to make eye contact, which is something new and troubling. His eyes follow the people walking past, like a New Yorker trapped at a party with a boring guest, looking to trade up. I have the clear impression he doesn't want to be seen by his colleagues talking to me.

"Now, you'll have to excuse me, Rupert, I have some other people I have to talk to before everyone starts running to the airport."

This is really bad news. Worse than I thought. If FINCA goes into IFC's liquidation group, we will have passed the Point of No Return. What is the matter with these people? Why do they want to destroy FINCA? I need to go straight to the top, get a meeting with no one less than the president of the World Bank Group, Jim Kim. Caesar, our chair, met him at a reunion at Dartmouth, and so he has heard of FINCA. He's also a Brown man, for what that's worth.

The other thing I have to do is have a talk with Lady Macbeth. Tell her it's time to step up or step off. She needs to get IFC to take a leadership role in this process. KFW and FMO are helping us; IFC keeps fucking us. It occurs to me there could be an opportunity in this.

Lady Macbeth, is it possible you have an enemy at IFC, and that you are the real target here? Perhaps you want to think about stepping off the board before they liquidate us. That would be the end of your post-retirement career as a board member on one or more of IFC's investees, you must realize that. Think about it: no more free trips in business class around the world; the end of your $35K-a-pop board fees. You might have to go back to work, set up your own "Trading".

Before I leave the conference, I debrief with Orsino, our Africa Regional Director, who wants to know if I had any luck convincing Theo to unfreeze our projects in Africa. I give him the bad news. He gives me the sympathetic "you're dead meat" look everyone does these days.

"Sorry, man."

That evening, Benvolio calls me from Washington to tell me Iago and Lady Macbeth want to revive the "succession" discussion. At least he called me this time.

"I think you ought to negotiate a severance package with them, Rupe, while you still have the leverage," Benvolio advises me. "Something like three or four years' salary. Otherwise, you could come away with nothing."

Negotiate a deal to give away control of my own company? I tell Benvolio what I heard from Theo at the conference.

"All the more reason you should get out now, Rupe. They want you gone. You'll never have more leverage than you do right now."

"Ben, we're talking about my life, here. I can't just walk away and let them destroy FINCA!"

"Rupe, we're talking about one year, here. It's not about who comes away with the heavyweight crown. You're going to continue to play a role on the board, in the worst case scenario."

"If I step down as CEO, their next move will be to get me off the board. Their goal is to take control of the holding. We can't yield on anything. Every time we make a concession, they just take it as a sign of weakness and ask for more."

Benvolio chuckles. "Rupe, do me a favor. Step back and think about this. Promise me you'll at least consider it."

"I'll think about it. And, Ben—" I am feeling emotional, suddenly. The words catch in my throat. "—I appreciate your sticking by me through all this shit. Seriously, you've been a great friend."

Although it's past one, I have another call to make, to Portia, our head of Capital Markets, who says she urgently needs to talk to me about Ecuador. I want to duck it. I've had my surfeit of bad news for one day; one more exploding worry bead and I may just book an appointment for a lobotomy. I hear operations of all kinds are dirt cheap in South Africa. They will even tack on a safari, free of charge.

Portia thinks I need to go to Quito and meet with our prospective buyers.

"Freddie is still waffling. The De Miro Bank guy downloaded all our data from the Due Diligence Room but now isn't returning my calls."

"What about Alfonso?"

"I'm beginning to suspect he's mentally ill. He's proposing that he pay us zero upfront, and in lieu of a down payment he will buy several million-dollar CDs from us. In return for that, he wants to take full control over the management of the bank immediately."

Fabulous. A turtle, an unethical Viking (maybe the only kind they have) and an escapee from a *manicomio*.

"All right, I'll go. Ask Rocky to get us a meeting with the Superintendent on November 30. Let's hope we have something by then."

INTERVIEW WITH A HYRAX

I dream I am scrambling on my hands and knees across a narrow ledge atop a high building, pursued by faceless men and baying hounds. One of the men overtakes me, and I start punching him, my blows landing on his chest with all the stopping power of kitten's paws. I leap from building top to building top. I come to a dead end, and, turning around, see all the other buildings have disappeared, leaving me isolated and alone. Change of Scene: I am in some kind of school, being pursued by a bunch of adolescent gang members. Each time they catch me, they let me go, laughing at me, urging me to run again. Catch and release with Rupert.

I awake at exactly 3 a.m.—F. Scott Fitzgerald's Dark Night of the Soul. Outside, moonlight floods the Stellenbosch, glittering like quicksilver over the ponds and illuminating the slopes of the mountains. This place truly is beautiful. No wonder the Dutch and English stole it from the Africans, driving them up into the mountainsides so they could occupy the verdant valleys. Today is our last day in South Africa. Going to the Cape of Good Hope. I could use some.

The Cape of Good Hope is a two-hour drive along a winding coastal road running south of Cape Town with spectacular views of the cobalt blue ocean far below. It reminds me of Big Sur. The drive is taking longer than expected and Lorraine is nervous about getting back to the vineyard near the airport, where we have a lunch reservation before our long flight back to London. At last the Cape swings into view: a paw-shaped promontory stepping gingerly into the smashing rollers of the South Atlantic. A narrow path leads from the crowded parking lot to the vantage point, a forty-five-minute walk.

"That's an hour and a half altogether."

"I'll just go halfway. Take a few pictures and double back."

Lorraine gives me a skeptical, warning look.

On the way, I come upon a Rock Hyrax munching on a crop of wildflowers growing alongside the path. The Swiss believe that if you spot one of these guinea-pig-size rodents your luck will change for the better. I remember my promise to Lorraine.

"What do you think, little fellow? To come 10,000 miles and not go the last few hundred yards?"

The Hyrax lifts his head, glances towards the Cape, then back at me.

"Go for it, mate."

Ten minutes later, I am standing at the tip of the Cape and watching the gulls glide across the glassy face of a breaking wave. I feel I have come to the end of a journey. I hand my iPhone to a fellow hiker and ask her to take my picture atop a rock, arms lifted, Rocky-like.

Eight rounds under my belt. One more to go.

NE ME QUITO PAS

---

4 a.m., two days later, in the Avianca lounge in Bogota, Colombia, with the other vampires, I watch the sky redden over the Andes, awaiting my connection to Quito, Ecuador. A bad news email from Rosalind is waiting for me when I switch on my iPhone. One of our important lenders to Ecuador is refusing to renew two million in loans when they roll over later this year. This squeezes down our precious liquidity. When the other lenders hear about this they may panic and follow suit.

I don't need this bummer the day before my meeting with the Superintendent of Banks. If he learns of it, he may reject our recovery plan. I could return home worse than empty-handed.

That night, I dream I am back in Bethesda, sitting in my easy chair in the family room. A physical therapist sits on an Ottoman before me. She seems to be preparing to administer some kind of leg massage. A voice offstage calls out to me, telling me I have just fifteen minutes before I have go somewhere. I question the therapist as to whether I have time for a massage. Ignoring me, she removes my shoes and the brace on my arthritic left ankle. She lifts my legs and puts my bare feet up behind her ears. This is getting interesting! Her nose crinkles up. "Mr. Scofield, when's the last time you changed your socks?"

I awake to find Lorraine has sent me an email from London: "Thinking of you and hoping for a god outcome."

A "God" outcome is probably just what is needed.

The Super keeps us waiting for over an hour in the conference room off his office while his Deputy, the *Intendente,* scrolls through spreadsheets on her iPad. It's a crystal clear morning in Quito and from the window we can see the *Volcan Pichincha* on the horizon, a column of frozen steam rising from its crater. Suddenly, the door to the office opens and a short man with a thin, manicured mustache enters the room.

"Christian Cruz. *Mucho gusto.*"

After a round of handshakes, Cruz asks me what I want to talk about. I tell him I am here with just one message: that the shareholder, FINCA Microfinance Holdings, is standing by our bank and is prepared to inject another $3.5 million in capital.

Cruz smiles. The tension drains from the room. He has been as nervous as we were, I realize, probably thinking we came to tell him we are pulling all our money out of Ecuador, as many other foreign investors have done recently.

"This is good news. And I have good news for you, as well. I am approving your recovery plan."

Rocky winks at me, an ocular high five.

"That said, I still see a difficult path ahead for you back to profitability. If you still want to sell the bank, let me know. I can help you find a buyer."

I thank Cruz for his offer to help. No need to mention here that Freddie the Tortuga has once again missed our deadline for delivering a binding offer. Freddie and Alfonso will no doubt be disappointed to hear the Super has approved our recovery plan. We are not out of the woods by any means, but we have bought another twelve months to effect a turnaround. I keep waiting for Cruz to bring up the dreaded "I" word. Apparently it's off the table for now.

Back on the street, basking in the warm, equatorial sunshine, I see Rocky is grinning at me.

"Estas feliz, no, Rupert?"

Yes, that's it! I am happy again, for the first time in months.

Lesson Learned Swag Box No. 18: Sometimes Ya Just Gotta Say Fuck It

Rocky pissed off Horatio, our CFO, and some other people when he forced the issue of committing to the Super that we would put in an additional $3.5 million in fresh capital. Horatio wanted him to try to persuade the Super to give us a waiver, but that might have been the straw that prompted the Super to pull the trigger on the intervention. Sometimes, you have to take decisions without consulting the rest of the team, if you suspect they may veto them. The Latinos call it *Mejor pedir perdón que permiso* (Better to ask forgiveness than permission). In this case, it probably saved our bank.

That evening, we repair to an Italian restaurant to celebrate our victory. Although it is half past eight, we are the sole patrons. The wine list has been severely depleted by President Correa's latest attack on the elite: doubling tariffs on imported booze. My favorite Chilean wine, Montes Alpha, *se acabó.*

Correa's grand revolution, without $100 per barrel of oil to fuel it, gasps on the sand like a beached blowfish. *El Jefe* is losing his appeal, even among his core constituency, the poor. Correa behaves as if nothing has changed. He spends half the municipal budget to build a metro for Quito. 600,000 central government employees get a big raise. To cover the deficit, Correa stops paying the government's vendors, including hospitals and clinics that handle the overflow from the Social Security system. When the hospitals started turning away the refugees from the public system, Correa sent in the police to shut them down on bogus health violations. Correa has borrowed heavily from his new friends, the Chinese. Wild rumors circulate that he sold them the Amazon basin, where all the oil is, and even the Galapagos Islands.

These days, autocrats, democratically-elected Heads of State and CEOs of big companies all have shorter lifespans. Everywhere you look, yesterday's heroes have become today's villains. The once-mighty BRIC countries, look at them now.

Dilma is hanging by her polished nails in Brazil; Jinping not looking so invincible in China. Only Putin, riding higher than ever, seems to have figured out how to spin economic straw into political gold.

This being *annus horribilis,* we get only halfway through dinner before Horatio calls to give us a balloon-bursting news flash: another one of our lenders to Ecuador is demanding repayment of a loan we had expected them to renew. Worse, they won't let us repay them from the Holdco, which means the repayment will attract Correa's capital repatriation tax of 5%. Together with the other loans we have to repay this month, the total hit will be $125,000 to our liquidity. Good thing we didn't know this when we met with Cruz.

A DREAM OF DAYS GONE BY

I dream I am with some childhood friends from Levittown, Long Island, my home town, at a corner gas station, dressed in Bermuda shorts and a tee-shirt. One of my friends points at my bare legs. Looking down, I see my legs are covered with ticks, swollen white with blood. I pick them off, one by one, but each one I remove is replaced by ten others. A terrible thought runs through my head: How long have they been there? Long enough to infect me with Lyme's disease?

With Ecuador back-burnered for now, our attention shifts back to Azerbaijan. A consultant we hired to provide an independent review of our recovery plan predicts we will get back to profitability in the second quarter of 2016, barring another negative external event. *Barring another negative external event.* He recommends we not try to engineer a sale right now, as "everyone is trying to leave now", making it difficult to do any transaction, even at a deep discount.

More cause to smile. Our lenders have insisted on this third opinion of our plan, assuming the consultant would conclude FINCA was being too optimistic and we needed to make deeper cuts to our staff and overhead. Instead, he has endorsed the current path and enhanced our credibility.

Horatio delivers more good news: we made a profit at the Holdco level in October! Only $200,000, but a positive number nonetheless. Upon closer scrutiny, most of it is accounting black magic, a reversal of $2 million in provisions resulting from

$4 million in loan restructuring. But if it holds up, and the restructured loans don't go back into arrears in the months to come—both what we economists call "heroic assumptions"—we get to keep it. This, plus the news from Ecuador, puts us—and me—in a much stronger position ahead of the FMH board and shareholder meetings next week.

Let the City be filled with joy and sacrifices!

In a tactical move, I decide I will pre-empt Iago and Lady Macbeth's latest plot to do me in by gaining approval of my succession plan from the FINCA International board, which meets the day before the FMH board. I'm being cute, but, technically, it is a FINCA International and not a holding company decision. The foundation still employs all the staff of the holding through a management contract.

My ruse works. Both the foundation and the holding approve my succession plan. Rosalind and I will serve as Co-CEOs for all of 2016, after which, on January 1, 2017, Rosalind will become the president and CEO of FMH while I remain as a board member and president of the foundation. From that lofty perch, I will remain the Supreme Commander of the entire FINCA Family, although this is a nuance I hope will go unnoticed by the shareholders.

The rest of the FMH board meeting doesn't go as well. Prince Hal, who serves as our most reliable messenger from the minority shareholders, tells us that: "Until Rupert actually disposes of a subsidiary, they won't believe he is even trying to effect a sale. So their position has not changed. Rupert needs to go, and immediately."

It's a lie, of course, but although we are close to a deal in El Salvador, until the ink dries on the sale of our subsidiary there, I am not free to disclose it.

After the FMH board meeting adjourns, Benvolio takes me aside, urging me to "focus on the foundation", which I take to mean he wants me to step down as CEO of the holding and "avoid the whole restructuring process, which is going to be agonizing." He says I should do this to protect my legacy. I listen politely. I don't give a fuck about my legacy. I need to save FINCA.

Lorraine has a turkey dinner awaiting me when I arrive home, around 7. I don't tell her we had turkey for lunch at the board meeting. After thirty years of marriage, you learn to keep your trap shut about some things. Lorraine has a kinder take on Benvolio's counsel: "Maybe he just wants to spare you from something he sees as going to be really brutal and risky for you."

That night, I dream I am driving my car and the transmission falls out. I get out to inspect the damage. The transmission cover is made of plastic, like a Clorox bottle. I keep trying to put it back in place, but every time I fit it back on it falls off again.

Lesson Learned Swag Box No. 19: Succession—No One is Eternal

Put a twenty-year gap between yourself and the heirs you are grooming. This way the organization will have two decades of leadership to fill the gap after your departure. And don't limit it just to the CEO, but develop it for the entire management team.

HERE COMES SANTY CLAUS

The year is winding down. Just one more ordeal to get through: the shareholder meeting on December 18. Perhaps the holiday season will mellow the temperament of my tormentors. Don't the Muslims forgive all their enemies at the end of the year? Then, on January 1, they get back to business as usual: sawing their heads off.

At first, there are propitious smoke signals from the other side. The agenda for the meeting arrives, and while "succession planning" is on it, the topic is "Division of Responsibilities for the Co-CEOs". Does this mean they have surrendered on the immediate elevation of Rosalind?

Second, I have a call with Osric, our new Chief Investment Officer at IFC, in charge of the FINCA relationship, and he cannot be nicer. He is in Jakarta, and tells me FINCA ought to consider working there. Turning to business, I tell him I have heard disturbing rumors circulating in the market that "FINCA is going bankrupt", and that the source was identified as "an international financial institution". Osric professes total surprise. He promises he will look into it and, if true, "this should be quelled immediately." He says he is also surprised to hear that his minions in the field are saying that they want to work with FINCA but can't "because we are being blocked by IFC Washington." Osric says "this should not be the case" and that he will make inquiries as to what is going on. He doesn't bring up the issue of "succession", or even the "Co-CEOs".

Could it be that the beheading sword has been lifted from my neck and I will be allowed to focus on fixing FINCA, without constantly having to look over my shoulder?

Perhaps, at the core, these investors are a simple lot. Just make money and they leave you alone.

Then, just as quickly, the Grinch drops a bag of coal on my head. Bad news from Ecuador: Freddy's board of directors met last night and decided not to make an offer. Ecuador is too risky, they decided, to invest in a bank. A year's work ends in nothing. I do a quick check-in with the Vikings and with Alfonso. The Norsemen are still in no hurry, and Alfonso puts yet another outlandish proposal on the table. It's clear he's disappointed the Super took the intervention pressure off us.

Today we give Rosalind a big raise in honor of her being promoted to Co-CEO. Rosalind is awesome. A single mother of two, with the World on Her Shoulders. Rock on, Roz! My own shoulders are rounded and stooped from bearing the weight of FINCA these past twenty years. A joyous burden, to be sure. I, too, must rock on, in my lowercase way. Continue the journey.

Kate, my current deputy, has also been promoted to Executive Director of the foundation. When I first made her the offer, she was terrified.

"I'm not ready!" she cried. "What if I fail?"

"You're ready," I assured her. "Besides, I have no choice. The board of the foundation wants me to put a dedicated team on FINCA Plus. Otherwise, they think the foundation will struggle financially once we separate from the holding. I agree with them."

FINCA Plus is the appellation we have given to our new line of business in non-financial services like renewable energy, water and sanitation, education and healthcare. After three decades of focusing exclusively on microfinance, FINCA has decided to go "holistic" and find creative ways to meet our two million customers' other needs. Since FINCA has no expertise in these other sectors, we plan to partner with social enterprises that do. I'm excited about this new vision. Among other things, it will take my mind off the fact that my shareholders are trying to destroy me.

This morning I skirmish with Lorraine over my travel schedule. She had signed us up to go to Costa Rica for a week at the end of January but hadn't put it in my calendar, so my EA just went ahead and booked me to be in Pakistan and Afghanistan that week. Who wouldn't prefer the two most dangerous countries on Earth to a beach week in boring old Costa Rica?

Tonight it's dinner with the shareholders, which should be a good portent of what tomorrow holds. But when we arrive at the restaurant, no shareholders. A text pops up on my phone from Prince Hal:

We decided to skip dinner and have a business meeting instead.

SPROING!

The morning dawns cold and gray, Mother Nature handling the stagecraft. We get a preview of what to expect when Osric asks management what we are asking in terms of support. I respond that we need the IFC and the other shareholders to help us keep the lenders on board, as they are jumping like frogs from a pot of boiling water. We could use an emergency line of credit. Equity should also be on the table. Osric, rejoicing over his newfound leverage, says they want to provide all this, but that it will subject to "certain changes in governance which are needed to modernize FMH and bring us to FINCA 2.0."

This is new. So IFC, the most dysfunctional bureaucracy on the planet, is going to teach FINCA a thing or two about governance? Can't wait to see what "modernize" entails.

Halfway through the day, the shareholders go into an executive session, without management. I spend the next two hours in my office, staring out the window, watching the cars and trucks dodge each other on Thomas Circle. The traffic pattern on D.C.'s roundabouts seems to have been designed by the body shop cartel. I count ten near-accidents in the space of an hour.

"Rupert, they want you back in the meeting."

I re-enter the conference room. Everyone avoids eye contact. Mercutio takes me aside.

"They came after Caesar," he whispers.

"How so?"

"Cornwall accused Caesar of 'a failure of oversight'."

"Did they discuss the Co-CEO arrangement?"

"Of course. They hate it. And Rupert, in your place, they want Rosalind to hire someone from outside to be COO." Mercutio smiles. "They have a number of suggestions."

Lorraine and I are heading up to our dacha in the Berkshires for the weekend, so after the meeting concludes, I don't linger. On my way to the elevator, I walk past the conference room. Our shareholders are all still there, seated at the conference table. Some wear broad grins; others are openly laughing. They have the look of a soccer team, flushed with victory. Prince Hal, our presumed ally, enters the room. He's likewise jocund.

CHARTWELL IN THE BERKSHIRES

Our beloved dacha, how I have looked forward to this! On the stressful, seven-hour drive to upstate New York, I imagine Uncle Vanya standing on the deck to greet us, arms open wide. What should be a happy arrival is marred by my inability to locate the key. In one of my many tricks for neutralizing my failing memory, I carry a ring of keys to our properties in my laptop case, but the one that fits in the dacha door is not among them. We keep one in a magnetic box beneath the deck, but it's not there. Lorraine and I accuse each other of having misplaced them. The truth is, neither of us can remember who had it last. In desperation, I crawl beneath the deck over the mouse droppings and—*voila*—find the key box where Jesus, our remodeler, moved it from its usual location.

After a few drinks, Lorraine falls asleep quickly. I can't sleep, still troubled by that scene in the conference room. Is Prince Hal a double agent? He seems too good to be true. On the drive up, I had a call with him, Caesar and Rosalind. Prince Hal advised us to insist on the Co-CEO arrangement, but just "explain it in a different way". He thinks we should yield to another demand the shareholders made, that we reduce the current board from eight to seven members. This means we would have to kick someone off from the FINCA side. He doesn't say as much, but I can guess he means Caesar.

The more I think about it, the more I am persuaded that Prince Hal is a German Kim Philby. It just doesn't add up. He's waiting for his moment, winning our trust and then, once we have come to rely on him—KABLAM!—he drops the hammer.

In fact, there is a simpler explanation, which I come to realize in time.

The next morning, the first snowflakes fall, fat, wispy ones. Jesus arrives in the late afternoon, on his way home from Camden, Maine to Western New York for Christmas. He's stopped by to walk us through the latest renovation plans. He did a beautiful job on our cottage in Camden so we hired him to fix up the Chatham dacha as well. In the course of the tour, we happen upon a dead mouse in the basement. Jesus's autopsy reveals the cause of death: ingestion of insulation foam.

"And the motive?"

Jesus frowns. "Assisted suicide. Or maybe just hungry."

MERRY FUCKING CHRISTMAS

We think the year has delivered enough bad news, but, just three days after the shareholder meeting, the Central Bank of Azerbaijan devalues the Manat by another 32%. That makes a total 65% for the year. In a reprise of its previous messaging, the government suggests that the customers of the banks appeal to the banks to repay their dollar loans at the old rate.

We are screwed. This means even bigger losses for FINCA Azerbaijan. *Sayonara* 2016 recovery.

In our final Restructuring Group call of the year, we discuss how to deal with the latest demands of our shareholders.

"Folks, let's face it," says Hotspur, our chair. "If it comes down to caving in to the shareholders on the 'Rupert Thing' vs. Mutually Assured Destruction of FMH, we're going to cave."

I can't believe Hotspur just threw me over the side. And with Prince Hal on the phone.

It's playing out *exactly* as I foreshadowed three months ago. Later that day, Rosalind drops a further rock on my head, saying she heard from Iago that he feels she must hire a COO because "the shareholders feel that existing management has failed and they need to see new faces."

That evening, Mercutio calls me to say has just spoken to Benvolio, who told him that Iago called to brief him on what happened at the shareholder meeting after the FINCA board members had run to catch their planes.

"The shareholders are going to demand that Caesar steps down as chair of FMH and Rupert resigns immediately as CEO. Benvolio was obviously feeling me out as to where I stood. I told him that my position is unchanged. No one has given me one good reason why Rupert should resign, other than 'He suffers from Founder's Syndrome.'"

Mercutio tells me he will do whatever I want, but if we cave he is convinced it will be the end of FINCA as we know it, and the IFC will seize control.

"And if Rosalind doesn't think she will be next, she's very mistaken. Lady Macbeth will be giving her orders, and her first order will be 'Scrub my office floor and go for coffee, Bitch.'"

That evening, Lorraine and I get into a terrible row. "You should have had that meeting with the head of the World Bank already! Now it's too late!"

I know she's right, but I just can't take any more criticism. I awake at 4 a.m., tormented by the dark scenario about to unfold. While Mercutio's words of solidarity are heartening, I suspect he knows the deck is stacked against us. I want to fight, but the pressure is going to be crushing. And how about my colleagues at FINCA? Will they really back me in a battle that could end in the destruction of FINCA and the loss of all their jobs? And would I want to really risk that outcome?

Maybe Benvolio is right. I should go quietly, focus on the foundation. Kate has overcome her self-doubt and is embracing her new role with enthusiasm. Take a step back, Benvolio says. Look at things without emotion. How would it play out? Caesar and I resign, the shareholders demand that Rosalind takes my place, putting them in control. Rosalind seemed exuberant yesterday, after her call with Iago. So I put all my energy into the foundation and—what?—just watch as Rosalind and her team try to make the save? I walk the halls, like Banquo's ghost, a guest in my own office, everything going on around me. Gritting my teeth as Rosalind shuts down our subsidiaries, one by one. To be sure, it will be a relief to be out of the pressure cooker. But how will I feel, reduced to observer status, helpless to influence the direction of the organization it took me thirty years to build?

The smirks of the shareholders in my conference room haunt me still. I picture Iago and Lady Macbeth, entering my office, triumphant smiles on their faces. Iago gives me a patronizing pat on the shoulder. "You'll survive, old man." Will it even still *be* my office? I imagine Lady Macbeth counseling Rosalind: "Shouldn't you be moving into Rupert's office? I mean, you're the CEO, now, not Rupert."

Step back.

Fuck that.

I have lunch with my old friend Alex Counts, who is a week away from stepping down as president of the Grameen Foundation, which he created twenty years ago. I helped start Alex on his career thirty years ago by giving him a reference for his Fulbright Scholarship to Bangladesh. His official version for retiring is that "it's time for a change".

"You want to spend more time with your family."

Alex gives me a sheepish grin.

"I guess the effort involved in raising $20 million each year just kind of wore me out. You have to be constantly replacing your major donors. Especially the guys from Silicon Valley. They'll give you a million a year for five years and then suddenly call you up and say: 'I'm done.' That and the amount of work it takes to manage a young, feisty staff."

"Tell me about it."

I think of how Rosalind is relishing the thought of finally realizing her dream of being CEO. She has the energy, the drive and the ambition to fill that chair. She will be a very different CEO than Rupert. More risk averse, less adventurous. Pleasing and responsive to the shareholders. She will unflinchingly, dispassionately close many subsidiaries, including Haiti and Afghanistan. She hasn't even been to most of the subs, not even once, so it will be easy for her.

Bitter, Rupert? She was your choice, remember.

It sickens me when I think of all the effort that went into turning Haiti and Afghanistan around. To fire all those hard-working staff, close the doors and walk away. Unlike other markets, few people will rush into those countries to fill the void left by FINCA. Who will take care of our clients?

Iago is right. I do suffer from Founder's Syndrome. And I'm fucking proud of it.

On Christmas Eve, I get a call from Caesar.

"Look, if you guys want me to resign as chair from the board of FMH, I have no problem with that. Mercutio could take over."

"I think that's a bad idea, Caesar."

"And you may actually want to turn over the helm to Rosalind at this point," says Caesar, trying to be helpful. "You don't need all that pressure at this stage of your career. You'll remain on the board, of course."

Maybe. Or maybe that will just whet their appetite for even greater concessions. To me, their end game is clear. They want Rupert totally out of the picture. It looks like Benvolio, Hotspur and now Caesar see that as inevitable.

Merry Fucking Christmas.

THE OYSTERS ANSWERED NOT A WORD

We fly to Seattle on December 25 to spend the holidays with Julie, Trevor and the grandkids. I am doing my best to get into the Christmas spirit despite the dark, malevolent nimbus hanging over me and FINCA. Last night, I awoke at 3:15 a.m. and did my usual twenty minutes of meditation, hoping to banish the demons spearing me in the ass with their pitchforks.

Calls with the Restructuring Group do not respect holidays. The one I take in Seattle is freighted with bad tidings. The minority shareholders have sent Caesar a "nastygram", the content of which is congruent with what Iago described to Benvolio:

Replacement of the Legacy Co-CEO and succession of the chairman of the board, given the evident lack of oversight. FMH needs to progress and keep pace with the current marketplace.

Rosalind offers to craft a response to be discussed at the call we have two days later. Rosalind sends me a draft, which I feel is far too conciliatory. I mark it up, turning it, basically, into a "fuck you" letter. Rosalind is dubious, but lets me present it to the RG, which is unusual since she generally takes the lead of late. I am only a few minutes into it when Prince Hal jumps on it, calling it "a total mistake", predicting the shareholders will be infuriated and the distrust between us exacerbated.

"I will be very blunt. Whether it is true or not—and personally I do not believe it is true—the shareholders do not believe the turnaround will succeed if Rupert is left in charge. And the way this is written, it looks as if with the Co-CEOs there will be a senior partner, Rupert, and a junior partner, Rosalind. At the minimum, I believe Rosalind needs to be in charge of the relationships with the lenders and shareholders."

Thanks for letting me take the bullet, Rosalind. The girl is learning.

It goes downhill from there. On the board issue, Hotspur makes the horrifying suggestion that we should let the minority shareholders put one of their people on as the ninth member to fill the current vacancy. By my count, this would give them a six-to-three majority over FINCA. I am assuming Iago, Lady Macbeth, maybe even Benvolio and Hotspur could vote against me if they think it's better for FINCA if I surrender. I wait in vain for Mercutio to object.

Then Polonius, our normally taciturn General Counsel, unexpectedly comes to my rescue:

"Let's not send the shareholders anything in writing. Based on experience, anything we write is bound to be misinterpreted. Let's thrash this out in a face-to-face meeting with a smaller group in early January."

I love this idea. The others concur. After the other board members ring off, management stays on to discuss whom we want from our side at this meeting. Rosalind stuns me by proposing that it should be Iago, Lady Macbeth and Prince Hal.

"Are you mad? The first thing they will do is throw me over the side. No way! It needs to be Mercutio, Hotspur and Prince Hal."

Rosalind mutters something to the effect that "it would be better if no FINCA people were at the meeting."

There is a less innocent explanation: she doesn't want to be Co-CEO, and probably never did. She sees Hotspur as her ticket to ultimate power. And she can count. The votes are there.

I recall another Christmas day, thirty-five years ago, when Ginny and I were breaking up. Ginny had gone up to NYC with Julie and was staying with a friend on the Upper East Side. I rented a white beard and red suit and cap from Lorraine's mother's costume shop and drove up Route 95 from Washington D.C. to surprise my two-year-old daughter. On the ride up, kids in the other cars pointed me out to their parents, shouting in delight: "Look, Mom! It's Santa Claus!"

When Ginny opened the door and I made my *Ho! Ho!* entrance, Julie ran screaming to the back of the apartment.

The Ghost of Christmas Present courts troubling parallels to those dark days. A sense of inevitability is setting in. Everyone feels it—the board, the shareholders, management, even me and Lorraine. How much longer can Rupert hold out? Mercutio says he will do what I want. I hear the unspoken qualifier: even if the situation is hopeless.

Lorraine points out that this was really my plan all along: hand off FMH to Rosalind and the foundation to Kate. Why not accept an early hand-off?

Take a step back. Think about it.

I search for the bright side. Maybe this seeming disaster is a blessing in disguise, clearing the way for the next chapter of My Brilliant Career. Fate blasting me loose from my too-comfortable corner office chair, casting me back into the arena to face my next challenge. How else to stay young and relevant? Preferable to wasting away on a golf course in some gated community in South Florida with the other geezers.

I recall Winston Churchill, the day after his humiliating defeat at the polls: "If this is a blessing, it is certainly very well disguised."

Over the next five days, I indulge in the rustic pleasures of the Northwest. Coaster-size oysters, Dungeness crabs looking as if they would come back to life any second, and flagons of craft beer. Reading to Fordy and Lucy, then turning into a monster, chasing them around the house.

An email arrives from Rosalind:

I have to admit to you it is wearing me down. I feel like I'm constantly being woven into some spider web of stupid politics instead of doing the work that matters. My instinct is to sit down with the whole board and talk straight. The way I see it there is no way you can leave this institution until we've stabilized it and you feel like your legacy is intact. Nor, frankly, do I want to do this alone. As I said on the phone the other night, you see things I don't that are really key. I hope you feel the same about me. We don't always agree, but that's actually what makes us special. And I feel like with Hotspur, Mercutio and Prince Hal in particular we have the group we need to talk straight to us when we need it, and I trust them.

There, now. Aren't you ashamed of the suspicions regarding Rosalind you harbored the day before? I think about excising them from this manuscript, but then what would be the point of writing this at all? I must faithfully record all the feelings and actions, noble or shameful, of the principals, including myself. Otherwise I forfeit the author's trump card: The Truth.

I recall Malcom Cowley's brilliant summation of Hemingway's career:

He faithfully reproduced the hard countenance of the age.

I feel the upswing of the pendulum. This time, my decision is final, irrevocable.

I am going to fight.

PART II—COUNTERATTACK

Just one more day in this God-awful fucking year. On the long flight back to Washington, D.C. from Seattle I have an epiphany: This whole mess *is* my fault. No, I don't mean the losses FINCA is suffering, but the fact that I have let Iago, Lady Macbeth and the shareholders get away with tagging me—and now Caesar—with the blame for it.

I have been a lousy communicator.

Rather than put out my own analysis to explain where we are and how we got here, I have made the classic mistake of allowing my adversaries to control the narrative. As a result, I find myself permanently on the defensive, dissipating all my energy in anger at my adversaries and in refuting their specious arguments, not in public, but within the claustrophobic confines of my own head. I have been marginalized, even by my allies, kept out of view "for my own good" as the mere sight of my face reminds the shareholders how pissed they are.

A new experience, I tell you. Akin to being black in the Deep South in the '50s, crushed by a tight belief system of racial myths and stereotypes impossible to contravene.

Okay, that was reaching. But it feels like the same thing.

I realize now the folly of my strategy and tactics, why they have failed so completely. In order to prevail, I shouldn't be relying on outwitting my adversaries to achieve short-term victories in minor battles and skirmishes, or consoling myself with the thought that, if all else fails, "we have the votes" to prevail in Total War. This will not take the day, and ultimately, as Hotspur predicted, we may break under the collective pressure of our shareholders and lenders.

Above all, I should not be relying on my allies—my fellow FINCA board members—to pull me through. Rather, I need to provide them with the munitions and weapons with which to vanquish the enemy.

I start by making a list of the false narratives and half-truths the minority shareholders and dissident board members are promoting, and develop an antidote for each.

1. *Rupert suffers from "Founder's Syndrome" and is resisting all the changes that need to be made to engineer a turnaround. He doesn't understand how the microfinance market has changed and is clinging to an outdated model.*

Far from resisting change, Rupert understands better than anyone that the microfinance market has changed dramatically since he made his first $50 loans to peasant farmers in Guatemala back in 1971. Today, the Legacy MFIs like FINCA face competition from predatory consumer lenders, credit unions, large commercial banks, telcos, payments providers, Fintechs and even utilities in the energy sector. To confront these challenges, Rupert has promoted a number of initiatives both within FINCA and the larger industry. Within FINCA, Rupert has been looking outside the organization to understand what is happening in the market and to see what other business models are succeeding in this new, more competitive environment. In the commercial banking sector, Rupert identified Metro Bank UK as a potential model for FINCA, and persuaded Metro's CEO to allow FINCA's management team to participate in one of its new employee orientation programs. Metro Bank is a UK clone of the hugely profitable and successful Commerce Bank, bought by TD Bank North in 2008. Metro Bank's unique "Surprise and Delight" and

"Turning Customers into Fans" approach to marketing now forms the basis for FINCA's Customer Experience program.

In the area of governance, Rupert is rebuilding the boards of FINCA International, FINCA UK and FINCA Canada with entrepreneurs from the financial and technology sectors. In the UK, Rupert has recruited three young tech entrepreneurs, under thirty, all of whom have built and sold companies in the social enterprise space and are bringing their experience and expertise to bear on the problem of global poverty.

In his ongoing search to identify new sources of revenue and breakthrough product ideas, Rupert has been attending conferences like the IFC's Fintech Conference in London, IFAD's Global Remittances Conference in Milan, and Mastercard's Symposium on Digital Finance in Cape Town, all of which have yielded valuable ideas and contacts for potential partnerships. He has supported the build-out of agent and mobile banking throughout the FMH network. In Pakistan, he is supporting the development of an app which could allow FINCA Microfinance Bank to leapfrog over the MFI-Telco partnerships and allow our customers to transact with us directly through the internet via low-cost smartphones, and without fees. Globally, he has challenged his 12,000-person team to come up with innovations that will help identify the winning business models of the future.

At the industry level, through the Microfinance CEO Working Group (MCWG), an alliance that was Rupert's brainchild and where he served as a founding co-chair, Rupert has catalyzed the collective resources of the ten major global microfinance networks to bear on the multiple challenges the industry faces, including figuring out how to utilize digital technologies to enhance the outreach and impact of the so-called "Legacy Microfinance Networks".

2. *Rupert views all of the subs as "his children" and can't bring himself to part with any of them, even those where FINCA has no chance of operating profitably or with scale.*

Rupert is leading the effort to sell the bank in Ecuador and made the contact with the prospective buyer of our sub in El Salvador. As a back-up, in case the effort to sell Ecuador fails, he put his best problem solver in charge of the bank, and he is keeping it alive. The El Salvador transaction is moving forward and has a good chance of closing.

3. ***Rupert is to blame for the situation in Azerbaijan, which went from earning $86 million over the past two decades to losing $15 million in 2015 alone. He should have foreseen the factors that led to this crisis, including Putin's invasion of Ukraine, the collapse of global oil prices which led to the severe devaluations of the Manat, and the interest rate caps which have crushed not only FINCA's profitability but that of the rest of the microfinance sector. Instead, he foolishly allowed Azerbaijan to build up a loan portfolio of a quarter of a billion dollars, financed with $50 million in equity and $200 million in external debt, creating the concentration risk that today threatens the very survival of FINCA's global network.***

In 2010, FINCA's CFO, Steve McGuire, warned against the high and growing concentration risk in Azerbaijan. In response, we lobbied the Central Bank to grant us a banking license which would have allowed us to mobilize savings and create a less risky capital structure. We recruited our partners—IFC and EBRD—to this effort. In Azerbaijan, however, there is an extreme prejudice against foreign companies, particularly in the financial sector. The only viable path to a banking license is to partner with an existing bank. For two years, we pursued this strategy, but were ultimately unsuccessful. Failing that, we made an effort to find a buyer for FINCA Azerbaijan. By then, however, the crisis was upon us, and no buyers could be found.

To manage the concentration risk, FINCA, led by Rupert, entered two large, underserved microfinance markets in Pakistan and Nigeria. We also invested heavily in growing our bank in the Democratic Republic of the Congo. Together, these three countries have a population of almost a half a billion people and could eventually provide levels of profitability and outreach that would easily offset the risk present in Azerbaijan and the rest of Eurasia. This strategy was working well until the external shocks struck, which no one had foreseen, including all the risk managers of all the financial institutions, including IFC, invested in FINCA.

4. ***Rupert and Caesar are guilty of a "lack of oversight" in that the board was not "systematically informed" of the level of guarantees/leverage and that there no policy to limit these.***

Total bullshit. Starting with the global financial crisis of 2008, the FINCA Audit Committee established and began enforcement of policies for guarantees and leverage at the network level. When FMH was formed three years later in 2011, these policies and enforcement practices were carried over from FINCA to the FMH Audit Committee. It's there on the record.

I feel better now. I email my eloquent Brief for the Defense to Rosalind and await her effusive praise.

And wait.

The next day I walk into her office and ask her how she likes it. She gives me a pitying smile, as she might one of her boys who brought her a half-assed homework assignment.

"I can see why you would want to put this out."

"But no?"

Slowly, she shakes her head.

"But if you ever write another book, you can use it for that."

Lesson Learned Swag Box No. 20: Fake News!

When John Kerry ran for president in 2004 against George W. Bush, he made a fatal mistake which ultimately cost him the election. Kerry, a Vietnam War Hero, allowed Bush, who used his connections to dodge Vietnam, to cast him as a coward in the infamous "Swift Boat" narrative. Kerry tragically assumed only a total fool would buy such a preposterous lie. Kerry did not count on the power of the False Narrative. Republicans, buttressed by Fox News and a legion of Hate Radio jocks, excel at the Art of the False Narrative, which they repeat ad nauseam until their prevarications are so deeply embedded in the public consciousness 100 tons of C-4 cannot extirpate them.

When things go south in your company, be on the lookout for the Rise of the False Narrative. Remember that your investors and lenders answer to retail lenders and investors of their own, and they are far more adept than you are since they have been through the drill many times before and know their fail-safe justification for their poor performance is: "It's management's fault." Don't waste a single day playing defense. When the False Narratives start to appear, swat them down immediately with the truth. You will find, as Jack Nicholson did, they can't handle the truth.

HAPPY FUCKING NEW YEAR

"I just spoke to Lady Macbeth about the meeting with the shareholders on January 11."

"And?"

"She's furious we won't be addressing the shareholders' issues."

"Like their demand to replace Rupert and Caesar?"

"Exactly. So I called the Prince Hal helpline, and Prince Hal is going to tell Lady Macbeth, sorry, the meeting will be about the lenders and only the lenders."

She's referring to an idea I had to convene all the lenders in Azerbaijan at an in-person meeting in London for mid-January. It's in lieu of my putting out my Brief for the Defense screed, which I have come to agree with Rosalind would be an exercise in futility. The purpose will not be to justify the past—and least of all defend Rupert's decisions—but to hear out the lenders' concerns and, if possible, get them to ratify our plan for the way forward. Later, Rosalind reports to me that Prince Hal reached a compromise where Lady Macbeth had to be content with getting my name taken off the letter we send the shareholders inviting them to the meeting.

I'm sure she means well. In Lady Macbeth's belief system, she is doing what's best for FMH, which is putting Rosalind in charge immediately so she can get sole credit for the turnaround. I can empathize. Lady Macbeth's years at the misogynistic IFC have left her irreparably scarred. She sees male-led conspiracies behind every bush.

That said, why would Lady Macbeth not see me as an ally in the whole *promote women* thing? I am keeping my promise to Rosalind to have her succeed me. Both my successors are women. Above all, I'm mystified as to why Lady Macbeth thinks that I suddenly have nothing to offer at this stage. Lady Macbeth once said to me: "The network you have created is amazing, Rupert." And what, the experience and knowledge that went into building that are now irrelevant to the turnaround? Hell, even Rosalind wants me to hang around. I shall have to ask her to explain this to me some time.

A little more than twelve hours left in 2015, *annus horribilis*. Look on the bright side, *amigo*. There were days when it looked like I would not survive at the helm of FMH a month, let alone the whole year. How does one celebrate the passing of such a year? A Hemlock Mimosa? Rosalind and I have been invited to Iago's annual New Year's Day gala. Lorraine wanted to take his wife aside and tell her that everyone is buzzing about his affair with Lady Macbeth. Steady down, girl, steady. I know it pains her to see what I'm going through. Such loyalty a man could never hope to find.

I think I will start dying my hair to purge the gray from my temples. I can't let the jackals see me as having aged this year, which I surely have. I dread thinking what's transpiring on the inside. So many mornings I awake with stomach cramps from the stress. Got to get more exercise. A New Year's Resolution!

But for the balance of this year, I fall back on my time-tested remedy:

Come, come, Mr. Bond. We both know you take as much pleasure in swilling as I do. Have another martini.

Lesson Learned Swag Box No. 21: Face Time in the Age of Technology

Despite Lady Macbeth's efforts to undermine me, I must credit her with some helpful advice she gave me: During a crisis, over-communicate. A corollary is: Whenever possible, do it face-to-face. I also have to credit myself for pushing for face-to-face meetings with both the shareholders and lenders throughout the crisis period. Even if sometimes the meetings lead to nothing concrete, I suspect they help to head off precipitous action on the part of our lenders and shareholders. It is easy to curse someone on email or Skype. More difficult when they are sitting in front of you.

A FRIEND IN DEED

I dream I am being chased by one of my daughters, although it's not Julie and it's not Michelle. Maybe some heretofore unrevealed offspring from my wild oats days? Whoever she is, I think she has a handgun, although I never actually see it, because each time I look behind me to see where she is, she tacks back and forth, obliging me to twist my head around and look over the opposite shoulder.

Change du scene. I am behind the cookie-cutter, Faulkneresque track house in Levittown, Long Island, where I grew up, beside an abandoned railroad trestle overgrown with weeds. There is a Homeland Security X-ray machine there, and the woman ahead of me, many months pregnant, is running one of her babies through the machine.

The morning brings an email from Prince Hal:

Dear Rupert,

I am actually still hanging out at a small New Year's Eve party, having just glided into the new year—but the curve on which women get more beautiful with every glass I drink has come to a sudden halt. And I can't get rid of my thoughts of FINCA.

Allow me hence to send you a few personal words about this part of my job, which has taken from me but at the same time given to me more emotional energy than all other parts, to say the least:

I am deeply honored to serve on the board of the last real microfinance network of this world. Maybe I cherish this honor of truly serving the poor even more than others in "my generation" because I joined the constructive side of international relations rather late, only at the age of thirty-three.

I am more than deeply aware of who created this—you at the foremost, and some others, several of whom today are being heavily criticized.

Let me reassure you that I am deeply convinced this criticism to a large extent is not fair. And sometimes in recent weeks I didn't feel well when having had to "transport" such criticism, which I deem at least to some extent unfair.

Please accept my excuses that I have done it nevertheless.

And please accept my explanations why I have done so nevertheless, e.g. in our call on Christmas Day:

In all my professional life I tried to retain a "hierarchy of loyalties" which goes: 1. The Mission, 2. The Institution and (only) 3. The Person / The Hierarchy. As a manager much more experienced than me, you know that such ranking is not always supporting career development, but it's part of my genes I am afraid.

And when looking at this, my hierarchy of loyalties, I must sadly confess that I cannot but apply this also to my role as FMH Director.

Seemingly, the minority shareholders have lost trust in your and Caesar's ability to lead through the necessary changes. Rest assured I have criticized this focus on persons since I came in mid-2015, but cannot stem the tide. It remains to be seen whether the lenders, many of which are linked to the shareholders, will look at it in a similar way.

As said above, this is certainly to a large extent not fair—but it is a perception. And it seems there is nothing more difficult than adjusting other people's perceptions—at least this is my experience in a life of "only" forty-eight years so far. For example, I couldn't change my wife's perception of my personality, and finally had to give up some time ago. Unfair, since perceptions most often are not open to reasoning.

But if perceptions—right or wrong—become a reality, and this seems to be the case here given the enormous needs for capital and funding in a good but probably overstretched network, the mission and the institution merit more attention than the persons acting. I am sure you share this belief, since otherwise you could not have created such an empire of doing good.

And adding to the perceptions' issue a reality certainly is as well that new minds and faces, which you already have allowed to grow in FMH, will find it easier to enact and project necessary changes than veterans who will always be associated with the battles and victories, but also the strategies and tactics of the past.

I am sure you will not try to fight stakeholder perceptions head-on, since this probably won't work and might only damage the mission, the institution and yourself. I am sure you have the sovereignty to include perceptions in your own planning, and make everything eventually fit into your own plan.

Honestly, I don't want to be in your shoes at this moment of time, and, frankly speaking, my major consolation remains that, if I'm ever at such a point in my career, the legacy I would have to smoothly hand over will be much smaller than yours.

My personal wishes for you for the next year, besides of course health and happiness for you and your loved ones, is that you may retain the sovereignty and leadership to decide for yourself which steps you take in the best interest of the good that you and some of your friends have created.

Rest assured I am not talking on behalf of someone else, e.g. the shareholder KfW. I just wanted to make sure you know where I stand before we assemble and jointly march into our "winter offensive".

Additionally, please believe me that I feel both obliged to and unwell at writing to you these lines—"obliged to" as I have explained, and "unwell" since I definitely play in a league much junior to yours.

Sorry for this unusual seasons' greetings.

Deeply respectfully yours,
Prince Hal

Seems I owe Prince Hal an apology as well.
I hastily reply:

Thanks, Prince Hal. Reminds me of one of my favorite Grateful Dead songs, New Minglewood Blues: "Couple a shots 'a whiskey, women 'round here start lookin' good."

I greatly admire your courage in taking an unpopular point of view when the easy thing to do would be to join the consensus. And no matter how this turns out—let's hope for the best—I will always hold you in high regard as a man of unusual integrity, and of course a great sense of humor which is always appreciated at times like this.

Believe it or not, I'm not unhappy in my shoes. In fact, I've spent most of my career in shoes like these, and as worn out as the soles may appear I think they still have a few kilometers left.

Happy New Year to you and your family. Don't let your wife pretend she isn't a lucky woman. It's worked for me for thirty years.

To which Prince Hal quickly responds:

Thanks Rupert! I salute both—the rank and the man. Yours, Prince Hal

So the endgame approaches. Do I detect a certain delinquent glee in Prince Hal's tone, and in the reference to the "Winter Offensive"? After all, he is a military man. Maybe he secretly hopes we, the majority shareholders, will mount a furious counterattack.

Dare we disappoint him?

To my delight, the lenders agree to meet, in London, on January 24. I get an added bonus: the shareholders agree to postpone any discussion of their infamous letter until after we've met with the lenders.

Lesson Learned Swag Box No. 22: It's Not About You
I am quite sure that if I pre-decease my dear wife, Lorraine, she will open the Memorial Service with the words: "This is not about Rupert." Subordinating my own need for redemption was key in getting the lenders and donors to shift their focus from venting their anger and frustration at FINCA and channeling it towards something more productive.

When in crisis, put your own needs last, and do what is best for the company. At the minimum, it will baffle your adversaries. At best, it may produce a better result for you.

By coincidence, Rosalind and I arrive at Iago's New Year's Day soiree at exactly the same moment. Iago's expression is quizzical, especially since I have not brought Lorraine, for the second year in a row. He tells me that he spoke to Prince Hal yesterday, who told him he had sent me an email. In this way, I am given to understand Iago knows Prince Hal advised me not to resist the pressure to step down. He also says that Cornwall has been reprimanded by KFW for his rude assault on Caesar at the December shareholder meeting.

"Cornwall is from the royal German bloodline," Iago adds, as if this explains but does not excuse his unruly behavior.

"I see. Well." We touch glasses. "To another interesting year."

Iago fills me in on some other intel he has picked up from his wide network of contacts. IFC has new leadership, a Frenchman, whom Iago describes as "Kim's middle finger to the IFC".

"IFC has studiously ignored the World Bank since Kim took over as president, three and a half years ago. This change could mean IFC returns to a more development-oriented focus versus just trying to make money."

"Inshallah."

"I know the new man, Philippe Le Houerou, well. Maybe that explains why the head of AFD, the French Development Agency, has asked me to help orient him in his new position."

That would explain it. Ah, Iago, we could have such fun with this were you and I on the same side! Perhaps we will be again. But first, I must convince you that I will be on the winning side.

Rosalind and I synchronize our exits, just as we have our arrival. Iago notices such things. He will report this to Lady Macbeth, next time she asks how Rupert and Rosalind are getting along.

The optimism I felt after the lenders agreed to meet with us chills in the cold January air. The more I reflect on the battles to come, the more foreordained the outcome appears: Rupert, Mercutio, Caesar and maybe Hotspur and Benvolio against the entire Development Establishment. How can we possibly prevail? As Benvolio suggested, maybe I should focus instead on what we can get in return for our submission to the Forces of Darkness. We should get something valuable in return, not just a retraction of their pledge to destroy us. Nothing for myself, but how about an investment in non-voting shares of $100 million, so that FINCA is not diluted? Framed this way, my capitulation would have a glorious sheen to it.

I ruminate on what Life Without FINCA would be like. Of course, presumably I would still have the foundation, but even so, I would be sidelined from the main action, and it would not be long—maybe a few days—before everyone on the staff and board of FMH started treating me like a recently deceased person. For that is what getting sacked is like: a form of death.

I remember when Ginny's father got sacked, after a long, mostly successful career in what he called "the rag business". It was the mid-'70s, and the relentless migration of the textile business, first from North to South, and then from the U.S. to the Third World, was approaching flood proportions. Charles made several trips to New York to fight with the unions, but was apparently unable to win enough concessions from them to keep his job. Getting fired so late in his life destroyed his self-esteem and, eventually, his health. He took a job as a stockbroker, just to keep busy, but soon after got cancer and was dead a year later.

Surely this will not be my fate. I will mourn for a while, but eventually I will get used to life on the sidelines. I will throw myself into FINCA Plus. After a while, I won't even miss the Big Time microfinance and the thrills and spills of trying to run a financial empire on four continents.

Okay, let's knock it off for the day. Do something exciting like change the air filters in the central unit, the hallway upstairs and the bedroom. Then watch the Redskins play a meaningless game against Dallas, where they probably won't play the first string. Have a few beers, drink some whiskey, and then smoke a cigar on the deck. Oh, and Lorraine wants me to help her take down the Christmas tree and stow the cushions on the deck furniture to prepare for winter.

Life without FINCA.

Inconceivable.

SUCCESSION BITES

Yesterday, at an All Staff meeting here at HQ, I officially promoted Rosalind to the Co-CEO position of FMH and Kate to Executive Director of FINCA Foundation. Fittingly, it was the first bone-cold day of the winter of 2016. Rocky was in town to discuss his contract, which will be another year at the helm of our bank in Ecuador. We have lunch across the street from the office and then take a stroll down 15th Street. I see Rocky glance at me every five steps. Finally, I stop and confront him.

"*Que es, Vos?*"

"*Te veo deprimido, Vos.*"

No fooling Rocky. After forty years, he knows me too well.

"Yeah, I guess I am depressed," I confess. "It's the first year we lost money at the holding. And it doesn't look like it will be the last."

"Ah, don't beat yourself up, *Vos.* It's business. We take risks. Everybody has a bad year or two."

"It's more than that. After thirty years building FINCA, I can see the day when I no longer will have anything to do with it. Much as I might tell people my involvement will continue, we all know it won't be at the same level. Slowly but surely, I will find my relevance diminishing until, at some point, people pass me in the hall and give me an *Are you still here?* look."

Rocky plants his finger in the center of my chest. "FINCA is your organization, *Vos.* And without Rupert, it won't stay on mission. So don't get silly ideas in your head."

The following day we have a call with the Restructuring Group to discuss our strategy for the lenders meeting. I wait for someone to broach the subject on all our minds, and when no one does, I force the issue.

"So what happens when the lenders make demands that bear an uncanny resemblance to those the minority shareholders are insisting on? And please don't tell me we don't have to worry because there's a 'firewall' between their equity and debt teams."

Prince Hal, realizing where I'm taking this, jumps on it.

"I think we have to take this up with the FMH board, and frankly, Rupert, you should absent yourself when we discuss it."

Nice. So that makes Benvolio the swing vote, assuming Hotspur votes with Mercutio and Caesar. I better have a call with him.

I actually sleep five hours that night, and peacefully. The next day, Rosalind tells me she's having a paranoia episode regarding some remarks I made at the All Staff, which she took to mean my heart really wasn't in this handoff and, worse, that I was having doubts about her ability to fill my shoes.

"Silly girl. You know I'm totally behind you and this transition. It was my idea, remember?"

Before she can delve into this, I change the subject.

"Mercutio and I have a confirmed meeting with a high-level official of the World Bank, for next Tuesday. Want to join us?"

"Yeah, for sure. What's the topic?"

"We're going to ask her to bash IFC on our behalf."

Rosalind gives me a "you're joking" look. She sees I'm serious.

"Maybe not this time."

"I thought you'd say that. Your momma didn't raise no fool, did she?"

Depending upon who wins the confrontation in London on the 26th, Rosalind can't have this get out, that she was present at a go-over-their-heads meeting at the World Bank. And what about me? I should probably dye my hair green and wear a mustache just in case someone from IFC spots me.

The next day we have a call with Responsibility, our biggest lender in Azerbaijan. They try to persuade us to meet with them in advance of the lender meeting on the 25th so they "can understand our plan for Azerbaijan and support you at the lender meeting". Nice try. Mercutio and Hotspur have given us strict instructions not to cut any side deals which would blow up the lender meeting.

"The Prime Directive is Treat all Lenders Equally," Hotspur reminds us. "Everyone has the same information."

I have a call with Benvolio, just to feel out where he stands. He seems subdued, doesn't try to sell me on resigning, which I take as a positive sign.

After work I buy fifteen Powerball tickets. The purse is $900 million, exactly the amount I need to pay off all FINCA's debts and buy out all our investors. I like the odds: 250,000,000 to 1.

I win $15 on an investment of $30. Doesn't quite get me there. But nobody else won, and the jackpot increases to $1.3 billion. I have a good feeling about this. I'm doubling down.

The meeting at the World Bank goes well. She says she wants to be helpful with our situation at IFC and is going to look into it, discreetly if possible. She is concerned, however, that by now "the situation may be binary" and if we delay taking action it may be too late. She is referring to what Theo alerted me about in Cape Town: that they may already have put us into the dreaded Work Out Group, a decision which might be irreversible.

I win $4 on a bet of $30 this time. Someone in California walks off with the $1.4 billion.

Lesson Learned Swag Box No. 23: Risky Business
Going over your investment officer's head in an organization like IFC is taking a chance that it may backfire and you will have created an enemy for life, plus made the situation worse. You also need to understand how organizations work, and that you can be absolutely certain

that the person you are appealing to is going to make sure he hears from the other side. We understand it would be extraordinary for a member of the World Bank Group to side with an investee against its own functionaries, especially given our miserable financial performance. At the same time, FINCA is a venerable organization with lots of allies in Washington, and we know we could make IFC pay politically if they took the decision to destroy us.

Only escalate when you feel you have exhausted all other avenues of appeal and literally can't end up worse off. You need to believe that your adversary is about to take action of his own that is going to destroy you.

An added worry bead: last night, for the third time in the past three months, I had a discharge of clotting blood in my urine. The first time it happened, I thought I was hallucinating, because the next time it was "all clear", literally, as if it had never happened. Then, last month, it happened again. Harder to think of it as an isolated event. I consult Doctor Google. A wide range of possible explanations, from too much exercise, to infections, to prostate cancer. Lovely. I wonder if it has anything to do with my hip replacement?

I call the doctor and make an appointment.

I speak with Madeline today, who works at IFC and was instrumental in helping us get the FMH deal done back in 2011. What a different IFC it was back then, all goodwill and supportive. Madeline is a friend, but pretty much marginalized from the FINCA relationship, which has been taken over by Osric & Company. Such a pleasure to be able to talk to someone who wants to hear the real story of what is going on, why it happened, and what we are doing to resolve it. Madeline says she thinks the shareholders will be pleased to hear I have kept my promise to initiate the Co-CEO arrangement. I don't tell her what they really want to hear is Rupert has been hit by a bus crossing K Street.

Madeline tells me there is also a "strong push" against Caesar, and asks me if "anything is being done about that". I say no and leave it at that.

I see Dr. Umhau, the man responsible for keeping me alive all these years. Dr. Umhau diagnosed my hemochromatosis twenty years ago, which, had it gone untreated, would have led to cirrhosis of the liver. The only known treatment is the equivalent of leeching: draining off a pint of blood every other month. Dr. Umhau thinks there is only a 7% chance my emissions are a symptom of something grim like cancer of the bladder or kidneys; more likely a popped vein leaking into my urethra. To be sure, he is going to put me through their algorithm, which unfortunately includes a date with Dr. Jeter and his weenie cam. It's set for the following week.

I dream I am captured by Nicaraguans and taken to an underground prison. The warden is a woman, maybe Lady Macbeth. A man, maybe Oswald, comes in.

"I'm very sorry, but we are going to shoot you."

I ponder this. Whom should I call? The Nicaraguans don't get along with the U.S. Embassy, so that's out. Wait a minute, this is not about them shooting me, it's about money. They want me to pay them a monthly stipend, and in return they won't kill me. This was the situation of someone my Peace Corps buddy, Jacobo, visited in a Mexican prison, who was serving a long stretch after getting busted for drugs. The first day, one of the other inmates come up to him and said: "You are a gringo. We know you have money back home. You need to have your family send you $500 every month. If you do, you will be fine. If you don't, you will have a problem."

NUMBING AGENT

The Restructuring Committee meets on the phone to plot how we want the meeting with the lenders in London to go down. Prince Hal is recommending that I don't go "because this meeting should be about the future, and Rupert represents the past. It really pains me to have to tell you this."

Mercutio refuses to go along with this.

"If Rupert is not there, everyone will say, 'See! Rupert is not even here for this very important meeting! He must be irrelevant, like the minority shareholders say!'"

Prince Hal is not happy, but he yields to Mercutio on this point.

We take up the question of how to respond to Cornwall's year-end poison pen letter to Caesar, in which he accused not just the Chair but the entire board of FMH of being derelict in our duties. I have come to see this guided missive actually as a gift, as it has the potential to galvanize all the board members against him. Mercutio recommends that in our reply to this letter we should think of how it will look as Exhibit A in a lawsuit against the shareholders—or them against us—if it comes to that.

"Further, if, as I suspect, the shareholders are out poisoning the lenders against us, and they decide to take a hard stand and say they won't cooperate with us unless we agree to every 'requirement' in Cornwall's letter, we call their bluff, say no, and dare them to demand repayment of all their loans. If they do, they destroy not only FINCA Azerbaijan, but also Ecuador and Russia. They will have to explain to people that they did this because they could not wait eleven months for Rupert to resign and for Caesar to step down as chair. The entire microfinance community will then know just how stupid and dangerous these investors are."

Prince Hal blows a fuse. He begs Mercutio to reconsider. He doesn't realize it's a double bluff, and Mercutio knows Prince Hal will share this with the other shareholders.

The following day brings the dreaded assignation with my urologist. As he preps the weenie cam, he asks me how things have been since our last encounter.

"2015 was a difficult year for me and FINCA. For the first time in our history, we lost money."

"Hah. Must be going around. We got robbed of $300,000."

"WOW!"

"Sorry about that. Sometimes the numbing agent works, other times not so much. Our office manager stole it. Who would have known? She had great references!"

The best of possible outcomes! No cancer of the kidneys or bladder, not even stones in either of those organs. Dr. Jeter's theory is that a blood vessel has ruptured and this would account for the periodic emissions. He gives a prescription he thinks will take care of it.

I dream I am in a capacious outdoor amphitheater, every seat filled with spectators. We are not watching a play. We are not watching an athletic event. We are watching someone digging up a pot of money I buried there some time ago, to finance a project I was working on. Why did I bury the money? Maybe I didn't trust my finance department. I know the beneficiaries of my project, many of whom are in the amphitheater, will be upset about this, seeing money intended for them get stolen. After the digger departs (and leaves his shovel), I go over and replace the money with a check from my own pocket. I return to my place in the top row of the amphitheater. Something feels wrong. I realize when the people discover that the money has been returned, they will assume the Bad Guy who dug it up has replaced it. I will not get credit for it. This is not acceptable. I rise and inform the 10,000 or so people gathered in the amphitheater that it is, in fact, my money buried in that hole.

The preparations for the big pow wow in London are in full gear. The financial model crashes the day before we are to travel to London. All the work the finance team has done for the past month dissolves in a hail of crazed electrons, all seeking—what? Other crazed electrons. Horatio and his team stay up until 3 a.m. to glue it all back together.

We gather in London for the Main Event. The venue we have chosen for this managed altercation is the Royal Academy of Chemistry, which seems fitting. You have to admit, the Brits know how to leverage their historical infrastructure. Our expectation is for a hard meeting where the lenders will demand to know how we plan to give them their money back. We don't have a good answer for them.

In Azerbaijan, our main problem, things have grown worse. Facing the public's wrath, the head of the Central Bank proposes to allow all microfinance clients with loans under $5,000 to repay them at the old, pre-devaluation exchange rate, i.e. at a discount of 50%. He says he has calculated the cost at $250 million. Cost to whom? Does the government intend to pick up this little goodie? He's silent on this point. It's a dumb idea on many fronts. For one, what about the people who borrowed $5,001 or above? Would they get a discount on the first $5,000 as well? If so, add another billion to the tab. Oh, they wouldn't? Better reinforce the gates of the Presidential Palace.

When you are an authoritarian dictator of a petro state, it's mostly upside, but not when the price of oil drops by 75% and shows no signs of recovery in the near term. Then, suddenly, you have no levers to pull. You don't have the liquidity to buy off your enemies. And since, in your arrogance, you told the IMF, the World Bank and all the other international financial institutions to fuck off, you don't have anyone to bail you out when your reserves drop to a paltry $5 billion, having spent the lion's share of it in a fruitless effort to prop up your plunging currency. Tsk, tsk. Fire those advisors who told you: "Mr. President, we don't need the IMF. We have oil."

Oh, I see. All your advisors are part of your extended family, and who wants to face the wrath of all those women when their husbands find themselves out of work?

This morning, while Caesar and I are in the hotel restaurant in London, Prince Hal enters. We wave him over. He gives us the "I'll just get a coffee" sign, loads his tray with pastries and then joins us at the table. I ask him how he thinks it will go down tomorrow.

"I think it will result in a decision to wind up Azerbaijan, which will produce big losses for the lenders, after which they will propose that the shareholders invest more capital in FMH, which can be used to repay them."

Not a gram of hesitation. This is not speculation, but solid intel based on a "pre-meeting" of the lenders and shareholders. Minus FINCA.

This additional capital injection to FMH would result in a major dilution of FINCA's ownership, in all likelihood below 50%. This would put the minority shareholders in control, resulting in the immediate and full implementation of Cornwall's "shareholder requirements", including "removal of the Legacy Co-CEO and current chairman of FMH".

Game over, in other words. Thirty years' work, up in smoke. But there is one caveat. Thanks to the genius of Caesar, FINCA would have to agree.

"If this is the case," Prince Hal continues, his breath redolent from a recent ciggy break, "then I think we should ask for something in return."

"Such as?"

Prince Hal glances at me, rips into an almond croissant, chews a moment.

"Speaking for KFW, we are awash with capital and might agree to co-invest at the country level."

"Why doesn't KFW do that anyway, without agreeing to bail out the lenders?"

Prince Hal gives me a sharp look, as he might a child who should have learned his lessons.

"KFW usually follows the lead of IFC. We've been in so many thousands of deals together, I doubt we could break that mold."

At that moment, Rosalind enters, dressed to the nines, looking ravishing. She tosses her blonde locks to clear her smiling face. We invite her to fill the empty seat, but she declines.

"Sorry, I have an appointment for a manicure. How are you guys?" she asks, checking each us in turn, trying to read our moods.

"We are good," says Prince Hal. "Strapping on our Kevlar and oiling our weapons."

I don't always put the pieces together as quickly as I did in olden times, when I was younger and more mentally nimble. But I do, eventually, put them together. Like realizing, an hour or so after Rosalind came into the restaurant, all dolled up, on her way to a manicure, that the reason she seemed nervous was that she was probably having that manicure with Lady Macbeth, who would pump her to divulge Caesar, Rupert and Mercutio's strategy for the board meeting on Tuesday. Which I doubt she would do.

That evening, my daughter Michelle (she lives in London) and I go out to an early dinner. We talk about the different dramas playing out in the Scofield and Innocent clans (the latter being her boyfriend's family). Michelle is writing again, and reads me a short story she is working on. I feel jealous. She surpassed me long ago, and is far better than me at being able to define a character in a single line, such as where a divorced father is picking up his five-year-old daughter "with her weekend backpack, stuffed full of colored plastic horses, each with its accessories".

I have been happy for the past few days. Part of it is the clearing up of my medical issue, but there is also an equanimity resulting the passage of power—and responsibility—to Rosalind and Kate. They aren't perfect. They aren't ready. But who is ever "ready" for this world, this life?

CHEMICAL WARFARE

We convene in the Science Room of the Royal Chemistry Society Building. It's a full house, with forty representatives of our seventeen lenders present, as well as the board of FMH, my whole management team and the top management of FINCA Azerbaijan. Rosalind, Horatio and I sit at a table facing the audience. I whisper to Rosalind that it has the feel of facing a firing squad. She gives me a wan smile. Lear takes a seat in the front row, as if to ensure he won't miss anything.

We have agreed that Rosalind and Horatio will take the lead, and that I will keep my comments to a minimum, except to answer any direct questions. Rosalind barely completes her welcoming remarks when Lear rises.

"Rupert, you are too old to run FINCA. You should resign and make way for new leadership!"

He rambles on for a minute or two, about how I have failed to downsize the staff and close subsidiaries. The other lender representatives exchange knowing smiles or, embarrassed for me, stare at the floor. Rosalind waits to see if anyone else is going to take the bait. After an awkward silence she says:

"Okay! Let's look at the preliminary results for 2015."

The results suck: we lost $12 million last year after eking out a tiny profit of $3 million in 2014. Azerbaijan contributed a loss of $16 million, single-handedly accounting for our atrocious financial performance. Does everyone get that?

Rosalind is followed by Horatio, who goes into more detail on the financials, and then the Azerbaijan team takes our places before the firing squad. Our CEO in Azerbaijan tries to make a case that FINCA Azerbaijan can still survive as a going concern. Several of the lender reps push back, arguing that we should immediately begin to wind it down, that this would allow them to recover more of their outstanding loans. Then the inevitable question comes up, from the representative of PROPARCO, the French Development Agency which had the misfortune of lending us $8 million a few weeks before the government capped our interest rates, crushing the entire microfinance sector.

"And is FMH planning to put in more capital?"

The team looks at each other, and then at me and Rosalind, to see who wants to catch this grenade.

"Not at this time," Rosalind responds, smiling bravely. "We simply do not have the cash."

"Why don't you then raise more capital from the shareholders?"

"We discussed this at our shareholder meeting, and there is no appetite for doing another capital raise at this time."

One by one, the other shareholder reps weigh in, pointing out the dubious case for FINCA Azerbaijan surviving as a going concern in the absence of a large capital injection. Mercutio and Prince Hal chime in, pointing out that, at the current level of monthly losses, which are at $3 million, any fresh capital the shareholders put in would be immediately be vaporized. None of the lenders say it, but they are all thinking "Not if you used it to repay our loans!" There are representatives of our six minority shareholders in the audience, including IFC, but they are all from the debt side, not equity, and they remain silent.

After lunch, the lenders ask that management and the FMH board members leave them alone to deliberate amongst themselves. This is the moment of truth. We know what they are discussing: whether or not to accelerate all their loans. If they choose to declare us in default, then the dominos will begin to fall, one by one, until FMH goes into liquidation.

We go outside into the sunny courtyard. Prince Hal and Rosalind fire up their ciggies while the rest of us talk in groups of two and three. An hour or so later the door opens and Claudius, the representative of Responsibility, our largest lender with millions in loans to over a dozen of our subsidiaries, calls out to us.

"Okay, FINCA, all is forgiven, you can come back inside now." Would it were so.

But they have good news. They have decided, for the time being, not to accelerate. Further, as our Restructuring Group had requested, they have formed a Lender Group of five to represent all seventeen lenders, which will make the negotiation process far more efficient.

The Cape of Good Hope Hyrax has delivered. We have survived. For now.

After dinner, Rosalind, Prince Hal, Hotspur, Mercutio and Lady Macbeth and I go to a Karaoke bar. Rosalind and I do "Highway to Hell" by AC/DC. Prince Hal does a surprisingly credible "The Piano Man" by Billy Joel. Lady Macbeth mostly watches, a big smile on her face. Is it the Sauvignon Blanc or have she and I finally made peace? It's getting late, and we have an FMH board meeting tomorrow. Back at the hotel, Rosalind wants a nightcap. She's energized. We repair to the lobby bar.

"Didn't the team do a hell of a job?" Rosalind says. "I was so proud of them!"

"Yeah, they did great."

The following morning the FMH board, minus Benvolio and Iago, convenes at the UK branch of our pro bono law firm Covington & Burling on The Strand. Polonius, our General Counsel, is also with us and Benvolio and Iago are on the phone. The agenda is to decide how we respond to Cornwall's letter.

"I have absolutely no doubt that letter is laying the groundwork for a lawsuit," Hotspur says. "In it, they accuse this board of failing to exercise our fiduciary duty. If this whole thing goes south, they are going to sue us."

Benvolio and Mercutio agree.

"We should think of that letter as Exhibit A in FMH board vs. FMH shareholders," says Mercutio.

Lady Macbeth and Prince Hal don't read it that way.

"Counselor, how do you read it?" Caesar, our chairman, asks.

Polonius frowns. The letter also contains a threat on the part of the shareholders to not approve the continuation of the Management Services Agreement between FINCA and FMH, which would, effectively, cut off all our salaries. It was an implied criticism of Polonius's work, which our normally unflappable GC did not appreciate. We agree Polonius will write a lawyerly letter that puts Cornwall on notice that we reject his accusation of "a failure of oversight".

"I love it," says Caesar. "Fuck you and a strong letter to follow."

"We still have to address some of the shareholders' other points," says Lady Macbeth.

"Which are?"

Next to me, Lady Macbeth is madly trying to retrieve an email on her laptop. Ah, she has it. "Well, here is the response from Osric to Dan's letter on the Management Services Agreement. He says, I quote, that Dan's letter 'completely ignores the concerns of the shareholders', and he asks me to make sure I bring up the 'governance issues' at this meeting."

Hotspur shakes his head. "I think, frankly, management has done a brilliant job despite all the challenges they faced in 2015."

"At first, I was against the idea of the joint CEOs," Prince Hal rejoins. "But now that I have seen it in action, it works, and I have done a complete about-face and I support it."

Twin jets of steam issue from Lady Macbeth's ears.

Lady Macbeth and Prince Hal decamp, running for their planes, leaving the FINCA people alone in the conference room. Hotspur is smiling about something.

"Last night, after the karaoke, Lady Macbeth trapped me in the elevator and railed on Rupert for about a half hour. Finally, when I could take it no more, I told her: 'Lady Macbeth, I think this has all been decided. Frankly, I think you're pissing up a rope.'"

The next afternoon, I am in the Emirates lounge, about to take off for Dubai, en route to Pakistan. And from there, Afghanistan. Back in Bethesda, poor Lorraine is going stir-crazy under a two-foot snowfall. Wehawken road has still not made the Plow List.

"How did the meetings go?"

"Incredibly well. I survived."

"See, I told you. And you thought you were down to two lives."

"I was."

"Yeah, but you get a reset at the beginning of every year. Still, be careful. Don't do anything foolish, Mon."

I am enjoying Life again. I am back in the game. And, I daresay, at least right now:

Winning.

CRY OF THE HYRAX

We're doing well in Pakistan, thanks to a great management team led by Mudassar, a U.S.-educated banker with a calm, professional way about him. The bank was failing and severely decapitalized when we bought it back in 2013. It made close to $2 million in 2015. We are working with a Fintech company here called Finja that has developed an electronic wallet that is internet-based and free to the customer, unlike the way the rest of the banking sector operates via Mobile Network Operators (MNOs), who hold both clients and banks hostage to their high transaction fees. If we can pull this off, we will leapfrog over them and own the whole sector, giving lie to the buzz in the market that FINCA is a washed-up legacy MFI run by a has-been fossil named Rupert.

The following day we fly over the snow-capped peaks of the Himalayas to Kabul, Afghanistan. Lorraine sends me an email from Costa Rica to say the weather is fine and Wish You Were Here. Could I be anywhere more different than a palm-tree fringed beach in Guanacaste? I cancelled two trips to Kabul last year and I can't let Perdita and the troops down this time. FINCA Afghanistan was at Death's Door three years ago, having suffered a debilitating fraud perpetrated by our employees, who ran amok after we had to evacuate our CEO due to a kidnapping threat communicated to us by the U.S. Embassy. Perdita took over, fired all the crooks and made it profitable again. Does anyone ever hear about these unsung heroes like Perdita who work in these incredibly difficult, dangerous countries so that the hard-working women can get loans to build their businesses?

Meeting with the staff, I learn that IFC has screwed us again, wasting months of our time working on a loan guarantee only to have IFC HQ order the local team to stand down. This will cost us several hundred thousand in foreign exchange losses because we will have to borrow in U.S. dollars instead of Afghani, the local currency. What's up with IFC? In the Congo, we are still waiting for a technical assistance grant to put more agents on the ground so we can reach more clients at a lower cost. In Azerbaijan, they killed a forward that caused us to be caught short during both devaluations, costing us $2 million. They didn't even invest in latest capital raise in Pakistan, our most profitable subsidiary. I'm going to call Lady Macbeth out on this when I get back. As IFC's board rep, she needs to start earning her keep instead of devoting all her time to sawing the floor out from under me.

I'm staying at Perdita's safe house, which has the windows sand bagged off except for a one-foot space at the top where we can poke our AKs through in the event of an attack by the Taliban. It has a clear field of fire up to the roof of the four-story building across the street, which is where the Taliban like to perch when they make one of their monthly suicide attacks in Kabul. Perdita's body guard gives me a modified AK with a scope to play with before I turn in. Since my Year of Living Recklessly in El Salvador in '83 I really don't sleep well in a war zone unarmed.

OMG!

Incredible development. When I open my email this morning, this is in my inbox:

Dear Rupert and Rosalind,

I wanted to alert you to a call I received today from Oswald at IFC. (He had asked for a call on Monday but I am flying out this afternoon to Tanzania for a month and so we spoke today.)

He said he wanted to make a change in the IFC appointed FINCA board member. Didn't give a clear answer why but said IFC management is very concerned about FMH and gave me nonsense about protecting my reputation. My sense is they want to put in an IFC staff person who would be clearly representing IFC. You know I view my role as representing the best interests of the company (FINCA). I don't know if they are looking to put on someone from the Special Operations (workout) unit.

I said I thought this was a big mistake for IFC and for FMH, that I felt the two-year history I have with FMH and FINCA was helpful to the company and to bring someone else in now would be disruptive and unhelpful. I said I feel FMH is on the right path and some very significant changes are in the works which will yield results.

I have asked to have a call with someone higher up but I suspect the decision is already made.

Needless to say I am very disappointed, because I love the company and its mission, feel I am making a contribution to the board and want to continue to participate in the turnaround to make FMH successful again.

I expect to speak with Oswald this week and will keep you posted.
Lady Macbeth

One of my nemeses has been removed from the field? I offer this sly rejoinder:

That is a shame. I agree we are making great progress and to disrupt the team we have, despite some minor disagreements, can only set us back. If you think it would be helpful for us to intervene let us know.

In any case I hope you will drop by our office in TZ. I still remember (and have on video) your inspiring message to the team.

Best

To which Lady Macbeth replies:

Thanks, Rupert.

Sadly I don't think contacting Oswald would be helpful but let's see after my call with him. Will keep you both posted.

I remember our Tanzania trip fondly. I won't be in Dar but do plan to contact the team in Moshi and have been in contact with Issa and the local team. Maybe there are promising new clients in Moshi!

Warm regards,
Lady Macbeth

No, if I were her I would probably not want an endorsement from the man Oswald wishes dead. In a way, I will miss Lady Macbeth. She did truly care about the mission—probably why Oswald wants her gone. And at least she slipped the knife in face to face, versus between my shoulder blades. Question is, who will take her place? Is someone from Special Operations opening a manila envelope with my picture in it as we speak?

Meanwhile, here in Afghanistan, war of a more serious nature continues. At 2 p.m. today, a young suicide bomber mingled with a line of young recruits hoping to join the Afghan Army and blew himself to Hell (one can hope) and twenty other innocents to Paradise. Attacks occurred in three other cities around the country. The Taliban said: "We are strong. We can hit you anywhere, anytime." The ancient game of strengthening your hand in advance of the negotiations.

I dream I am playing a pickup game of soccer in some park, dribbling around trees and other obstacles and then putting the ball through an untended goal. I meticulously count my scores: three.

That morning, watching Al Jazeera on the tele at the safe house, the sports announcer reports that Ronaldo scored a hat trick for Real Madrid.

Should I be doing a victory jig? If Lady Macbeth is correct, then IFC has come down on the side of pushing for our liquidation. I don't think they can do it unilaterally; they will need all the other shareholders to agree. Prince Hal and KFW will disagree, as would, hopefully, FMO. From FINCA's side, it would mean Total War.

Today we go out to visit a branch near one of the markets in Kabul. Perdita has arranged a costume change for me, a Tribal Kit, so that I can move about unnoticed. Says my coloring is identical to one of the Northern Tribes from Nuristan Province, in the southeast. I do my usual routine with the guys at the branch, asking them to tell me what their biggest worry is. All the credit officers say it's the growing arrears, which worries *me*. Perdita tells me it's the bad economy, that a growing number of people have concluded they have no future in Afghanistan.

"And it's not the people fleeing the conflict areas in the South this time. It's people here in Kabul who have the money to pay people to smuggle them out."

Now for the part of my job I love the most: speaking with our clients. Most of our clients in Afghanistan are women, but due to the traditional Islamic culture they can't walk unattended through the streets, so we have to meet with them in their homes. We meet with a group of women who borrow money from FINCA to buy cloth, which they sew into blouses and dresses. The women have brought their children with them and one of them reminds me of my granddaughter. I buy a dress for my granddaughter, Lucy, similar to the one she is wearing.

We talk about the challenges the women faced when the country was ruled by the Taliban. The leader of the group tells us that life was intolerable.

"We never left our houses. We couldn't run our businesses. Our daughters were not allowed to go to school. Today, things are much better. There is more freedom." She adds, with a rueful smile: "Now all we need is peace."

Back at the safe house, zipping up my suit bag, I flash on what it would be like to close up a body bag. Or be inside one.

POOF

The financial results are in for January, a loss at the network level of $6 million. Leapin' Lizards, what a way to start off 2016! As usual, Azerbaijan accounts for virtually all of our losses, having shed $5.5 million *in one fucking month!* We have the government to thank for this: the president of the Central Bank, purported mouthpiece of His Excellency Himself, said in an interview with the local Jingo Journal that he thought it would be a good idea if the banks let their customers repay their dollar denominated loans at the pre-devaluation rate, i.e. at half their value. Imagine if President Obama, through Janet Yellen, had suddenly announced it would be "a good idea" if everyone in America's debt was reduced by 50%.

Into this furnace of bad news Rosalind strides boldly to lead our first telecom with the lenders since our meeting in London. She bravely announces that our goal in Azerbaijan is that "everyone will get their money back", meaning them, presumably, not us. A stony silence ensues, signaling their ... what? Endorsement? Incredulity? Come on, guys, say *something.* We all know, at this juncture, that the lenders have the same chance of coming out "whole" as an arctic seal held aloft in the jaws of a great white shark has of "coming out whole". Highly unlikely, good sir! But Rosalind makes them *want to believe it,* which is important in the early innings of a catastrophe. Rosalind deflects no less than a half dozen polite queries as to our plans to "put in more capital". Sorry, fellahs, there are absolutely zero plans to "put in more capital" because *we ain't got none!*

Wow, what a mess. Meanwhile, on the other side of the globe, in El Salvador, our CEO is resisting selling our business to Gustavo's MFI, Optima. Rosalind wants me to give him a call to "tell him how much we value him". Okay. "Dude, we value you so much we have decided to sell FINCA El Salvador and send you back to the States." I'll work on the messaging.

Rosalind tells me she had a call with Lady Macbeth, who finally had her face-to-face with the higher-up.

"The higher-up told her that IFC and FINCA appeared to be on a collision course and it was best they didn't have any IFC people on the board when the *Titanic* hits the iceberg. Lady Macbeth said she tried to talk him out of it, FINCA was making all the right moves, etc., etc., but he remains unconvinced."

"Shit."

"On the other hand, I spoke with Theo, and, for what it's worth, he said he is okay with the Co-CEO arrangement."

Well, IFC is a big place. They don't always talk to each other, even on the same floor.

I write these lines just as I have embarked on my second Bloody Mary, en route from London down to Uganda. I find myself, despite the January financial results, which have exploded in my inbox like a Taliban Madrassa-reared suicide bomber on the streets of Kabul, in a happy place, mentally speaking. The angry dialogue with the shareholders that ran in the back of my head like an anti-virus program all these months has diminished to an occasional spark of indignant vituperation, quick to sink back down. I think my time in Pakistan and Afghanistan lifted my spirits.

Or maybe it's the vodka?

Definitely losing it. Left my laptop at the hotel in Kampala; had to make frantic call to the hotel and have someone race out to deliver it to me at the airport. All ended happily (obviously).

Things remain tense in Ecuador and Azerbaijan. Horatio is in denial about Ecuador, and wants me to go down to Quito and persuade the Super to let us not put in another $3 million in loans and not be profitable in 2016. This would put us right back where we were at the end of last year, nervously biting our nails down to the quick to see if we could complete a sale or persuade the Super to let us operate as a going concern. Rocky and I just managed to do that, and now Horatio wants me to deliver a message that will in all likelihood have the Super reconsider an intervention. Horatio, please! What do you think I am, a miracle worker?

The emails on Azerbaijan keep flying like rabid bats. One of our competitors, Azeri Credit, reached out to us about a merger, then dumbed it down to an acquisition, and is now pretending they can make it on their own as a going concern. Our team is not wild about the merger idea, likening it to roping two torpedoed cargo ships together to see if they can sink more slowly. I suppose we could be accused of the same Magical Thinking? All depends on if our clients decide that it's pointless to wait for us to forgive 50% of their loans and start repaying again.

Had a long but good day with the clients out in Masaka, and then dinner with Patrick, our CEO, and his team. The women are going wild for these Bio-Lite stoves and our solar lanterns. Truly life-changing products, each for less than $100. They literally go from living in darkness to light, and from a prehistoric existence to living like human beings. I am excited about our new line of business. I just hope we live to grow it.

Patrick has the election weighing on his mind. Five years ago, there were several weeks of chaos in the run up to it. Museveni, the incumbent, says he's good for another fiver, but just in case, he's trying to put his opponent in jail. Is there any part of the FINCA network that isn't unstable right now?

OWERI (OH WEARY), NIGERIA

Regarding Nigeria, as a popular saying goes, there are two times when you feel sad. The first is the day you arrive, the second, the day you leave.

I love this country! Yesterday, we inaugurated our second branch office in the bustling Relief Market. They unveiled a marble plaque on the wall with my name on it. A thousand years from now people in Nigeria and Uganda will be asking, "Who the hell was Rupert Scofield?"

After the market visit, we have a meeting with the Controller of the Central Bank. She wants to hear our expansion plans, and, as always with Central Bankers, wants to know if we can lower our interest rate, saying she has "received a lot of complaints from your customers". I tell her that we will in the future, but for now we have to break even, and we don't have fresh capital we can put in, so it must come from retained earnings. She gives me a "heard that one before" smile. As we rise to go, she says she has one further question.

"Why did you chose Oweri?"

The question takes me by surprise. Usually, the Central Bankers tell me how they're grateful that FINCA has opened a bank for the poor in their country, especially when it is an underserved city like Oweri.

"What was that about?" I ask our CEO, as we walk to our car. He smiles.

"I don't know if you know this, Rupert, but Oweri is the money-laundering capital of the world. The Controller is probably curious why a company like FINCA chose this place among all the other locations in Nigeria with large, underbanked populations."

Now, suddenly, all the half-completed high rises in Oweri come into context.

"Somehow our team missed that detail in the feasibility study."

When I get home, after nearly a month on the road, I find a gracious email from Lady Macbeth in my inbox:

I am so in awe of what you created over thirty years. It has been such an honor getting to know and work with you. FMH now needs to change like much of the world but you created such a meaningful foundation. I am so grateful for the opportunity I had to work with you and your team.

Well, all right, not a bad outcome, all in all, I suppose. I just wish you hadn't expressed your awe in such unconventional ways, such as trying to get me fired. I try to reconcile such niceties with things like the infamous "elevator incident" in London, fail, and then I just toss it. One doesn't need to figure out all the quandaries in life.

Speaking of which, we still haven't responded to Osric's letter of last December. After our meeting in London, Prince Hal took it upon himself to try to engineer a meeting between a smaller subset of the FINCA board members, excluding Caesar and Rupert, and just IFC, KFW and FMO. Prince Hal's hypothesis was that if the "Big Three" could cut a deal with FINCA, then the single-digit shareholders would have to come along.

To Prince Hal's surprise, it is IFC who sabotages this maneuver. Osric is having none of it. He responds to Rosalind's and my invitation, copying all the minority shareholders we were trying to exclude, saying he doesn't think it is a good idea to meet with only a subset of the shareholders. Of course, the hypocrite sees no problem whatsoever in peeling off a subset of minority shareholders for his own back-channel plotting.

Poor Prince Hal. He's trying so hard. I will be interested to see how he takes being knifed in the back by Osric. To my chagrin, he blames it on Caesar! At our next Restructuring Group call, he says: "The chairman should have acted sooner after our board meeting in London to implement the plan." And Osric would not still have sabotaged it? While I am disappointed in Prince Hal, I understand his frustration. And he has done too much good not to forgive the occasional peccadillo.

Lesson Learned Swag Box No. 24: When Doing Nothing is the Best Course

Back in the '80s, when I was a union man and Cold Warrior, I worked with a Cuban named Rolando who was our Country Director in Ecuador. Rolando was a sugarcane worker who had been imprisoned after Castro took over and was one of a group of labor leaders rescued by George Meany and the AFL-CIO from an appointment with a firing squad. Rolando did not get along with Pedro Chavez, the Secretary General of the Ecuadoran Labor Confederation, who was constantly trying to persuade Rolando to turn control of his budget over to the Confederation. At a meeting I attended, this negotiation went on for over two hours, ending with no resolution. Afterwards, I asked Rolando why he and Jorge didn't come to any compromise. He told me these inconclusive meetings had been going on for over a year, all with the same non-outcome. "You don't need to solve every disagreement, Rupert," Rolando explained. "Sometimes, there is no good compromise. So you just keep talking."

The best example of this, of course, is the Israeli-Palestinian negotiations, which never have and never will

produce a solution. But we know from experience that when the talking stops, the shooting begins.

In the FMH shareholder dispute, we ultimately decided not to respond to Osric's letter at all. But we kept talking. And talking.

PART III—THE END OF THE BEGINNING

THE CRACK-UP

Today I have meeting of our SMART Campaign Steering Committee, which is a microfinance industry client protection initiative. We are making good progress, and have "certified" over fifty MFIs around the world serving over twenty million clients. To my surprise, I see Autolycus has confirmed his attendance. I didn't expect he would have the nerve to show his face in public after how he had defrauded FINCA. It means he is still in denial. I need to clear that up now.

I sit close to him, one empty chair separating us, so I can pick up any intel I can make use of later in our lawsuit. It doesn't take long for me to be rewarded. The guy sitting next to him asks how his fund is doing. "I'm struggling," Autolycus admits, his head swaying like a broom endeavoring to sweep up dust balls of sympathy.

At the break, he corners me as I am out in front of the elevators, finishing up a phone call. In an act reminiscent of John Turturro in *Miller's Crossing*, pleading for his life, Autolycus's eyes water up and he says, "I know you're angry at me, Rupert. Please, forgive me!" I almost expect him to add: "Look into ya heart!"

"We are in the process of preparing our complaint, Autolycus, so it wouldn't be appropriate for us to talk," I tell him, delivering the line Polonius, our General Counsel, has recommended I deploy in the event of such an encounter.

I am sitting up in a hospital bed in a windowless examination room. Lorraine is sitting in a chair a short distance away. She leans forward, staring intently into my face.

"Are you back?"

"What do mean, 'Am I back'? Did I go someplace?"

"This morning, you got up, took a shower, and then stood in the bedroom, looking confused. You asked me 'Why am I naked?' 'Because you just took a shower,' I answered. 'Where are my clothes?' 'You haven't put them on yet.' Then you looked down at your naked body, and back up at me, and asked the same questions again. About 1,000 times. Finally, I called Johnny, and we took you to the hospital."

The next day, I go to see Dr. Umhau, who had been filled in by Lorraine as to what happened. He doesn't seem that concerned.

"I actually know something about this condition. When I was recently married, my father-in-law had a similar experience. He was on the squash court, when suddenly he stopped playing. In his case, he just got in the car and drove home. Apparently, you can still function in this state; you just don't recall anything that happened."

"Maybe I was abducted by aliens."

Dr. Umhau doesn't miss a beat. "It's possible, I guess."

"Has it got a name?"

"Temporal Global Amnesia."

"Does it usually reoccur?"

"No," said Dr. Umhau firmly. "Only very rarely. You probably will never have an episode like this again."

Let's hope not. Is there anything more terrifying than the thought of losing your mind? I guess if you do, it doesn't really matter, does it?

Can one get used to losing millions of dollars every month?

We lost another $6 million in February at the network level. At this rate, we will lose $70 million for the year.

A near-death experience, i.e. near bankruptcy, is an essential part of the Entrepreneur's Journey. Just ask Elon Musk. It builds character. It humbles the arrogant.

But why does it have to happen in the first two months of the year?

The day begins with a four-hour long call with the shareholders, the first time we have spoken as a group since back in December. As expected, the yellow-bellied single-digit minority investors elect Osric to lead their jihad.

"FINCA has completely ignored the minority shareholders!"

"The past five years under FINCA's management have been completely wasted! The shareholders have received no dividends, and no exit!"

Mercutio lets him rant for about ten minutes and then says:

"Are you giving us a lecture or is this a conversation?"

Rejoins the Fool:

"Oh, is this Mercutio? Is this Hotspur? I'm sorry, but we haven't met."

Actually, you did, Osric. Several times.

Osric softens his tone a bit, going on another ten-minute nonsensical digression. He says the board, which we have agreed will be comprised of nine members, should be reduced to seven, and two of the FINCA representatives should step off, one to be replaced by an "independent" board member. It was Osric who insisted we expand it from seven to nine in the first place. We put Hotspur on immediately, increasing our majority from four-to-three to five-to-three. The minority shareholders rejected all our candidates for an independent board member, a search which took the better part of a year. Hotspur takes it as long as he can stand it, then cuts him off.

"Okay, Osric, let me summarize in five words what you just said in 1,000."

Benvolio's voice comes on the line:

"When I read your letters, I thought: 'These people are about to sue us!' Is that the way we want to go? Because if it is, then understand this is a one-way path; there is no turning back. But if we want to solve the problem, let's solve it. Let's talk about it. Let's find a solution."

After four hours of bullshit, we come out in exactly the same place as two weeks ago, when Prince Hal suggested a smaller group meet to settle our differences. Osric agrees to this, pretending it was his idea.

Why do we tolerate such types in our society? Better question, why do they rise to the top?

THE IDES HAVE IT

It has been only 2,060 years since Caesar staggered through the Forum in his blood-soaked toga with the Senators' daggers bristling like porcupine quills from his back. Some days, I can relate, Julius.

Poor Rosalind is encountering stiff headwinds with the Azerbaijan lenders, who can't agree amongst themselves whether to let FINCA Azerbaijan try to make it as a going concern or throw in the towel and move directly into a wind-up. Some think they will recover more money with the latter approach, others with the former. In either case, they need to sign a "Forbearance Agreement" in which they formally commit to not accelerating their loans in order to give us time to work things out. Some still can't get over the fact FMH isn't going to put in more capital. Others, like PROPARCO, want a side deal where they get paid first. There are seventeen different lenders to Azerbaijan and as many opinions as to what we should do. We have already lost all our capital, we keep reminding them. $50 million, to be exact. Everything we are trying to do is for your benefit, not ours. Please, make up your minds.

Sainte Rosalind. Such patience. Not a day passes that I don't thank my lucky stars Rosalind is handling these negotiations and not me. Some in our group think she's too patient, and what the lenders need is a good, stern talking-to, plus an ultimatum: Fine, you don't like the way FINCA is handling this? Here, the Keys to the Kingdom. Take them. You guys run FINCA Azerbaijan.

Prince Hal doesn't think Rosalind is too patient. Pretty much anything Rosalind does is fine with Prince Hal, I've noticed. Including joining him, outside, on his ciggie breaks.

And how do I spend my time? Today I go out to Oxford to give a talk to the students interested in International Development. At the end of my speech, a young man from Uganda stands up:

"I owe my education, and the fact that I am here, to my Auntie who paid my school fees with a loan from FINCA Uganda. I am so thrilled to meet the man, the president of FINCA, who has done so much for the people of Uganda."

Wow. I'm sure many in the audience think I staged the whole thing. How refreshing to be revered again, however briefly.

Things are moving inexorably towards the End Game. Since the lenders couldn't agree to accept our standstill plan and sign the Forbearance Agreement, we decided to go ahead and present our own standstill plan, which is basically to stop all repayments and put those that are falling due into an escrow account, from which everyone will be paid, pari passu, when—and if—the Restructuring Plan is approved by everyone.

This ain't going to be easy. One of the smaller lenders is playing hard to get and is, so far, the lone holdout. But they could be playing the "Bad Cop", in a strategy approved by the others, to wring more concession out of us. Responsibility is coming to meet with us next week on March 15 (with daggers?), and another gang of lenders on the 16th and 17th. Oh, boy. Shootout at the OK Corral.

Meanwhile, elsewhere in the network, the aftershocks of the Azerbaijan earthquake are making themselves felt. Lenders to our other subsidiaries, even the healthy ones, have added a new condition to rolling their loans: any of the fees we take which sustain FMH HQ must be subordinated to their loans. Wow! A clear tactic to starve us into submission. This will be a welcome development to our subsidiary CEOs, who have always groaned under the burden of the tribute paid to keep Rome afloat. Liberation Day! No more controls, no more annoying requests for reports and other information. In Kyrgyzstan, where we have been losing boatloads of money due to a devaluation of the Som, our CEO calls to say that the Central Bank is putting a moratorium on payment of dividends by money-losing financial institutions, and that she is "afraid that this could include payment of our Management Services Agreement with FINCA International". Coincidence? With the burden of the MSA lifted, suddenly her losses disappear. The easy path back to profitability. This is all we need, an unholy alliance between the lenders, the Central Banks and our own CEOs.

"You're paranoid, man," Rosalind declares when I spin out this conspiracy.

"I've earned it. Listen, *mi amiga*. We need to dig a series of trenches, the first of which we will certainly be thrown back from, but the last of which must be a fight to the death. For while some of our investors may want to see FINCA survive, others clearly want to recover their money by any means possible, including liquidation. They know there is still tremendous value in the FINCA network; their goal will be to extract as much of it as possible through sales and liquidations of subs. At the end of this process, FINCA will be no more."

Now I have her attention.

"Okay, just get me a shovel."

Today we meet with a consulting firm tasked with helping us restructure and cut our operating costs. Rosalind and Horatio hired them on the advice of our shareholders and over my strenuous objections. The partners in the firm are all castoffs from one of our competitors that abandoned microfinance and underwent a radical downsizing.

"You do realize they will be working not for us but for the minority shareholders, and at the end of this the shareholders are going to say, 'Why don't we just hire them instead of FINCA to manage FMH?' You do realize that?"

The consultants are already seated in the conference room when I enter. They have just come from IFC, and I can see in their eyes they heard an earful about Rupert. Obstacle to change. Defender of the status quo. Refuses to cut staff and "sell his children". I look forward to my one-on-one interview with them. I confuse them by telling them we need to put a radical option on the table: that HQ disappears and the subs operate independently. Five sets of eyebrows around the table rise in unison.

Later in the day, Polonius pokes his head in my office door with breaking news:

"I just got out of the Governance Committee meeting. Iago and Prince Hal are pissed at Osric and IFC for wasting the time of the Restructuring Committee! I think the FMH board is finally united! They are going to demand that IFC stop sending us people who can't make decisions."

Glad tidings!

But in FINCA, these days, glad tidings have the lifespan of a mayfly. This morning, the day of our board meeting, Mercutio tells us that he and Benvolio had met with Osric last Friday and that "Osric agreed to everything we said on governance, including the nine-person board. The only thing he insisted on was that we appoint an investment banker to the board to help with the footprint reduction."

"You mean like Alex, the guy you proposed over a year ago and who was rejected by Lady Macbeth and Iago?"

"Exactly. Then Osric made some remark about 'the first time I met Rupert he was with some "little girl", Rosalind, who he said would be taking over as CEO'. I told Rosalind that and her head exploded."

That night, Osric calls again. He tells Mercutio he met with his overlords at IFC and they disagree with everything he negotiated with FMH. That "nothing has changed, Rupert and Caesar are still there, and they need to go". It's kind of fun driving them crazy, I think.

"Why did we waste our time even talking to him?" Mercutio asks rhetorically.

At the onset of the FMH board meeting, Benvolio shares a groveling email he received from Osric, doing another 180 back to what he had originally agreed to regarding the expansion of the FMH board to nine members. Apparently, Prince Hal and Iago called their HQs in Frankfurt and the Hague and complained about IFC wasting their time with a rep who had no authority to cut deals. My friend, Oswald, who has been pulling Osric's strings, apparently got bitch-slapped by his boss and told Osric to cave. At the break, Benvolio comes up to me, grinning.

"We've got Osric back under his rock. We need to keep him there."

"I'll keep my foot on the rock," I promise. "And press down on it until his tail stops twitching."

Lesson Learned Swag Box No. 25: When Doing Nothing Isn't the Best Course

At some point in a negotiation, if the other side cannot agree, you need to take unilateral action and hand them a *fait accompli*. This will force consensus and enable you to stay in control. It's a better outcome for them as well, compared to stasis. Of course it will piss them off to no end.

CUT THE CORD, HE SAYS

Shit news from Nigeria on two fronts. First, the government announced they are planning to impose interest rate caps at 3% per month. Currently we are at 5%, and still losing money, so this will kill our business as interest rate caps did in Azerbaijan. At least they are giving us the chance to comment—a whole week of advance notice! The second piece of bad news is our CEO in Nigeria was found guilty of sexual harassment so we are going to have to sack him. Bad luck comes in threes. What else is out there?

Rosalind killed it yesterday on the Lender Steering Group call. She rattled off our position, the logic of it, the worse options available. She left them nowhere to stand other than to mutter "how disappointed" they were that we weren't shoveling fresh capital into the oven to be burned up. The price of oil has ticked up recently, shoring up the Manat and slowing the erosion of our remaining capital. We take some solace from that, but know it could be short-lived.

I have my differences with Rosalind—she's so quick to vote to shut subs down rather than fight to survive—but I have to admit it gives me comfort to see that she's really better than me at things like what we're going through now. Very smart, diplomatic, but hard-nosed when she has to be, and really taking charge of the situation.

I have lunch with a friend of mine, Let's call him CIS (my Companion in Suffering), who runs a social enterprise on the West Coast. He's known as kind of a kook in the industry, which

makes him a hero in my eyes. I share with him my travails with
my holding company partners.

"I went through something similar with the investors in
my fund," he tells me, "in Azerbaijan, of all places! They don't
behave like businesspeople, these international bureaucrats.
We had a big fraud and they all panicked. We could have
saved the company but we all ended up losing 50% of our
investment and the company itself went bust. They have no
patience, these people! They don't understand that investments in these developing markets don't only go up, they can
go down as well. They act like they're investing in a company
in Norway or something!"

"So it's not just me."

"I wanted to out the bastards, go public and reveal their
hypocrisy. This 'impact investing' where everybody talks about
a 'double bottom line' is such bullshit. At the end of the day,
they only care about the money, and people need to know
that. But a friend of mine on Wall Street talked me out of it.
He said they would sue me blind."

We say goodbye on the corner of 15th and Eye Street. But
first we take a selfie to put on Twitter.

I speak with Orsino about all the shit going down in Africa.
Pending devaluation and interest rate caps in Nigeria; crashing commodity prices in Zambia and the Congo; stagnation in
our sub in Uganda. In Uganda, Orsino is terrorized by Lear,
whom he thinks has too much leverage over us, to the extent
we have to cave on everything, including turning a blind eye
to the CEO who is wrecking our bank.

I'm frustrated today. I know it's part of this whole transition
thing where, day by day, I feel my power and influence over
FMH ebbing away. People don't advise me when meetings are
cancelled or changed. Significant decisions are taken without
consulting me. I have been THE MAN for twenty-two years,
and for all the headaches, it feels bloody strange to have to
make "suggestions" and "recommendations" instead of deliver

orders. And have those suggestions and recommendations often ignored.

Get used to it, boy.

It reminds me of a similar disempowering time when I stepped down as Executive Director of the Union program in El Salvador, back in 1984. I had only been in the job a year, but what a year! I learned more during those twelve months than in the rest of my life up to that time. It made me the leader I am (was?) today.

And my successor came in and trashed everything I had built.

As president of the foundation I will still have a big role, but let's not kid ourselves: the real action is going to be with FMH for several years to come, until the foundation re-establishes itself as a "playah" in the social enterprise space.

Meanwhile, Azerbaijan continues to occupy center stage in the drama that is FINCA. The lenders meet, separately, and Horatio reports they seem aligned around accepting a pari passu payout of our excess cash, on the order of $12 million. Our unilateral action approach worked. Hotspur advises Rosalind to first slap a bunch of conditions on it regarding them rolling their loans for the next two years or until we either throw in the towel or—by some miracle—FINCA Azerbaijan survives the crisis.

Meanwhile, we receive a visit from Lady Macbeth's replacement, Hanif, a banker who worked at IFC for twenty years, who has come for his "orientation". Hanif sits patiently through the first fifteen minutes of Rosalind's presentation and then, having learned all he needs to know, gives us IFC's prescription for returning FMH to profitability:

"You need to double the size of your average loan, Rosalind."

Rosalind gives me a quick look that says: Why didn't I think of that?

Afterwards, I escort Hanif down to the lobby.

"IFC believes that FMH is subsidizing the foundation, Rupert. I have orders to cut the umbilical cord between FMH and FINCA and cut it completely."

I am tempted to dash back up to the eighth floor and bring down a carving knife from the kitchen. I could tell him that the FINCA board feels the opposite is the case: FINCA has been subsidizing FMH. Maybe I'm going about this all wrong. Rather than fight a defensive battle against the IFC on my home turf, I should be taking the war to them on theirs.

Mr. Jim Kim, President
World Bank
Washington, DC

Dear Jim:

I'm sure that you, like me, recognize that the IFC has become a dysfunctional, soulless graveyard over-populated by Wall St. Washouts. Maybe it makes money, maybe it doesn't, but it certainly isn't having a gnat's wingbeat of an influence on World Poverty. So that is why I think you should consider replacing the current leadership with someone like myself. Or better yet, with myself. I therefore, with the utmost humility, enclose my c.v. in the expectation that you will give it your serious consideration...

I can just see myself, on my very first day, addressing the entire 20,000 employees through a jumbotron video conference connecting 230 countries:

Hi, guys. I'm Rupert, your new boss. I have a reputation for fairness, transparency and honesty, and that's why I am going to give it to you straight: I want every last one of you varmints to clean out your desks, go home and start packing. That's right, you're all fired, every last one of you.

Haha. Just kidding. Well, not in your case, Osric. And Oswald. And... let's see... I know I had a list somewhere... Ah. Here it is. Wow, more like a telephone book!

LET IT GO, LET IT GO

I decide to start "restructuring" my files for the time when I have zero executive responsibilities in either FMH or the foundation, and serve only as a board member of FMH and as president-for-life and a board member of the foundation.

I am about halfway into the process when an unsettling memory surfaces. It was the summer of '73, a few days after my father passed away at the age of fifty-five, following a long battle with colon cancer. I yielded to my curiosity and went up to his bedroom (really no more than an attic in our cookie-cutter Levitt house) and started going through the contents of his desk. As with most men who have served in the military (my father was Air Force, flying ninety missions during WWII over Southern Europe from his base in North Africa), my dad was meticulously neat and organized and the contents of his desk reflected that. In the center drawer were his knickknacks, two of which were familiar to me: a pen from an ocean voyage on the Cunard Line that had a miniature replica of the cruise ship in a water-filled glass bubble, and a piece of shrapnel from an anti-aircraft round Dad told me had narrowly missed his head and stuck in the ceiling of the bombardier cockpit. In the top left-hand drawer was a tightly packed file of correspondence—mostly bills and bank statements, leading back many years—but there were also letters going back as far as WWII and my childhood, which led me to conclude that this was the totality of my dad's incoming letter collection. Sorting through them, I found a letter from my Great Uncle John, who was offering to underwrite an operation "to fix Rupert's legs".

Fortunately, my father must have declined that proposal, one result of which was that I could blaze down the lacrosse field and roll dodge to my left with blinding speed, since my left appendage was slightly shorter than the right. The second was a reply from Joseph Heller, author of the mega-seller *Catch-22*, in which Heller told my father that he had not modeled the protagonists in his book on my dad's bomber squadron, although, he would allow, the B-25 crews and their missions probably had much in common.

So there it is, Dad's life, I remember thinking as I pushed the drawer closed, redolent with trapped time.

The same sense of closure haunts me now, as I go through the contents of my desk at FINCA. So many projects, deals, employees, crises, opportunities and, of course, hundreds of business cards have coursed through the past thirty years, and to what end? Many have told me they stand in awe of everything FINCA has accomplished. Maybe even I am in awe, just a little. But so what? Wonderful, we did a lot of good, and still are.

But what do I do next?

I won't be idle, for sure. But gone is that happy yoke of responsibility for all the big, important stuff that has been the center of my life for the past four decades. The thrill of getting up each morning, checking my emails, and wondering what happened in the empire over the past eight hours, while I was "off duty"? I could—and will—still check that every morning. But it won't be the same. Someone *else* will be responsible for fixing whatever horrific mess has befallen us, or for taking credit for some stunning triumph we have engineered against impossible odds.

This is going to take some getting used to.

Then there is that most terrifying thought: Did I make a mistake turning over the reins? Like the song goes, did I make my move too soon?

Then it hits me. Maybe what scares me most is I am giving up my POWER.

LOOK ON THE BRIGHT SIDE, BRIAN

It's not all bad, of course, I think as I shovel my entire drawer of performance evaluations into the dustbin. No more work plans to review! No more budgets to approve! Someone else to lead the preparations for the board and investor meetings!

Wow, I made a lot of changes to the top management over the past two years, I realize, noting the names on some of the files.

Lesson Learned Swag Box No: 26: When the Horse is Dead, Get Off

If your organization is successful, it means it is constantly growing, which means your top management is facing new challenges on a daily basis. Hopefully, they will rise to the challenge. But not all will. When you've tried everything—training, coaching, performance warnings—and nothing is working, don't shrink from cutting your losses and changing out a faithful, trusted manager for new talent. It sucks, I know. But never forget that you are not in control of this; your organization is. And if you can't bring yourself to do it, then don't be surprised when the board concludes that it's time to change you out.

LA VERDAD ESTA EN EL CAMPO

(THE TRUTH IS IN THE FIELD)

After the shareholder meeting, Rosalind tells me she wants to talk about troop movements. She feels Petruchio, our Regional Director for Eurasia, is not being totally straight with her—not just with Azerbaijan, but with the rest of Eurasia. She says she has heard rumors that he has been telling his people "not to tell Rosalind about all the bad things going on".

I share her worries. I have just performed an analysis of the delinquency in the Azerbaijan loan portfolio, and I have a bad feeling that Petruchio's reports to the lenders that we had "achieved four consecutive weeks of declining portfolio at risk" failed to caveat that this had been accomplished through a combination of write-offs and restructurings of the portfolio. My own analysis, which I did last night, shows that PAR 30 has risen by $6 million between February and March when these two "adjustments" are taken into account.

I tell Rosalind to stop agonizing and make some changes. Petruchio is a burnout case. He was supposed to go on a three-month sabbatical, but when Azerbaijan blew up he had to cancel it. Petruchio is also an insomniac and can't sleep without the aid of a healthy dose of Woodford Reserve. Much as I sympathize, it is the job of management on the ground to be the most pessimistic possible, otherwise we at the top of the house are bound to look stupid at some point. And how can we submit a restructuring plan based on a "positive trend" that is a fiction?

Shit, this is not a good development. My confidence, once shaken, becomes insatiable for data. Looking at the big picture, this is where we stand in Azerbaijan as of March 31, 2016:

Total Debt Owed to Lenders	$127 million
Total Loan Portfolio	$111 million
Total Current Loan Portfolio	$51 million
Total > 30 Days Past Due Loan Portfolio	$28 million
Total Restructured Portfolio	$32 million
Total Cash	$15 million

Our total assets—cash + loans receivable—adds up to $126 million, one million short of our total liabilities to our lenders. We are "light", as Tony Soprano would say. Under the Best Case Scenario—in which we recover 100% of our loans, even the past due and restructured—we are still "light" by $1 million. But really, all we can count on recovering with 100% certainly is the $51 million that is current, leaving us and our lenders "at risk" for a loss of about $75 million.

I'm feeling the need to go more hands-on in Azerbaijan; travel there and see for myself what's going on. Rosalind can't travel, pinned down as she is by her twice weekly calls with the Restructuring Group and weekly calls with the lenders.

In preparation for my trip, I decide to line up some high-level firepower. The IMF, I reason, must be preparing some kind of bailout package for the banking sector of Azerbaijan, and maybe I can persuade them to include microfinance. Kate, through her husband at the IFC, puts me in touch with the desk officer at the IMF who deals with Azerbaijan. I am pleasantly surprised to learn that, yes, microfinance is a part of IMF's agenda when they speak to government of Azerbaijan—next week, as it turns out. Do I hear the cry of the Hyrax?

On our next call with the Restructuring Group, the A&M team sounds glum.

"I don't think the lenders are ever going to reach an agreement, even on how to divide up the available liquidity," Chris, our A&M advisor, informs us, "let alone on any restructuring plan."

John, our outside lawyer, is less pessimistic.

"If we can just get a majority of them to agree on the plan, then they can force the others to come along."

Chris disagrees. "I think it's going to take FINCA just telling them, 'We can't do this for free anymore. Management is just spending too much time on Azerbaijan with no compensation. So we're going to collect our Management Services Fees and Royalties.'"

"That would certainly shake them out of their paralysis," John agrees.

We have three weeks until the next meeting in London, where we are going to provide the lenders with three scenarios: a Base Case, a Stress Case and a Liquidation Case. After I blew up Petruchio's attempt to persuade us that the PAR was declining, people are starting to coalesce around the gloomy view that FINCA Azerbaijan will never return to Going Concern status.

Two weeks later, I talk to my contact at the IMF to see how their trip has gone.

"We told them at every meeting that we believed the caps were a mistake, and that they needed to allow interest rates to rise again if they wanted to revive the economy. It seems there's this advisor to the president who has a lot of influence over him and has him convinced that they need to keep rates artificially low. It's ridiculous: the cost of bonds in the local market is 15%, leaving a spread of only 10% for operating costs, PAR and profit. Microfinance simply can't work at those levels. We told them, but they aren't listening."

I thank him for making the Old College Try. I tell him that pretty much dooms FINCA and the whole microfinance sector. No one is going to invest fresh capital under those circumstances, and the equity of the whole sector has pretty much evaporated. *Courage,* my contact tells me. The IMF's CEO, Christine Lagarde, is going to a conference in Baku at the end of May, and President Aliyev himself is rumored to be showing up.

I dream I am playing soccer. Or trying to. It is as if I am playing while wearing ankle weights. Each time someone passes me the ball, I move towards it, but another player comes along and strips it from me.

Change du scene. I am in Azerbaijan with the country's president, attending some kind of picnic. I keep trying to engage him in conversation, to ask him if he can do something about the interest rate caps so FINCA Azerbaijan doesn't go out of business and 300,000 people don't lose their livelihoods. The president doesn't seem to care. He stands up and leaves the picnic table; walks around in fretful circles, speaking to himself, half in English and half in Azeri.

The A&M boys complete their restructuring scenarios for Azerbaijan. They don't look pretty. Even if the lenders convert a good chunk of their debt to equity—which would have the double advantage of reducing our interest rate costs and making the operation more resilient—the lenders will recover more of their capital via a wind-up now versus waiting for FINCA Azerbaijan to get back to profitability. That's the impact of the interest rate caps, which have destroyed our business and the rest of the microfinance sector.

I speak to my friend Scott, the CEO of Vision Fund, who is also trapped in Azerbaijan and doing a slow bleed-out. He tells me the lenders are threatening to pull their loans in his other countries unless he absorbs a greater share of the losses in Azerbaijan. So the lenders are equal opportunity blackmailers.

Lesson Learned Swag Box No. 27: The Eyes Have It

No matter what business you are in, there is absolutely no substitute for seeing for yourself what is going on at the front lines. If you don't, your staff will quickly learn you will never see for yourself what they are up to, and they can literally tell you anything and you will have no choice but to believe it. On the other hand, if they know you could show up, unannounced, anywhere, at any time, they will be far less likely to get up to any mischief. I have never gone to the field and not gained important insights.

HAIL MARY ON THE CASPIAN

I fly to Baku, the smoking crater that is drilling through the financial heart of FINCA. I wonder if this will be my last visit to this country. Usually when the Boss arrives in town, it is a cause for celebration and lots of whiskey, cigars and expressions of thanks to the team for the great work they are doing. This time will be different. To be sure, regardless of what I find, I will feign optimism and express my faith that we can engineer a turnaround. We have to keep the morale up, even as the enemy has broken through the last line of defense and is bayoneting the wounded.

Soon after I land, I visit our branch in the main market on the outskirts of Baku. Normally places like this are teeming with traders and their customers, so many it's hard to navigate the narrow passages between the rows of shops. Here, the parking lot outside looks empty save for a few cars and customers making their way towards the shops.

We stop first at our branch office in a shopping center on the outskirts of the market. I am surprised to find all of our credit offers hanging around at the branch instead of out in the market, talking to our clients.

"We have stopped most lending," the branch manager tells me. "We spend most of our time on collections. Our clients aren't as happy to see us now."

85% of our loans in this branch have been restructured. I am told this was necessary due to our clients' inability to make the scheduled payments because of the slowing economy. The branch manager shows me the paperwork for a client with a $17,000 loan who is only able to make payments of $100 per month. Loans in Eurasia are much bigger than in Latin America or Africa. At this rate, unless his business recovers, it will take him fourteen years to repay us. I ask when they expect the economy to recover and business to pick up.

"Around September," the branch manager tells me, looking into my eyes as if to see if I believe this.

But when I go out to the market and start to talk to our clients, a more mixed picture emerges. The first is a shoe-seller, who, when I ask him if he is making money these days, tells me: "If I wasn't making money, I wouldn't be spending twelve hours a day here in this market." His small shop is piled high with shoes he has imported from Turkey. Our credit officer tells me his loan has been restructured so that his payments are more affordable. Another client we visit, in another part of the market, has two gift shops, one for the "regular people" and one for "ministers". The first sells souvenirs in the under $100 range. The second has garden ornaments and household furnishings which sell for as much as $6,000. The owner makes me a gift of one of his products, a handicraft featuring miniature Azeri string instruments. He says business is good. He has another business in downtown Baku. I find it difficult to believe this client needs to have his loan restructured. The same with a third client, who sells hardware. He tells us that if FINCA would finance him without requiring collateral, he could borrow us much as $300,000, which he would invest in three container loads of merchandise that he would sell right out of the containers at the edge of the market. His loan has also been restructured.

Querying the staff, it turns out that many of the restructured loans are done for clients who complain if they don't get the same deal as the ones who really need it. As usual, to find out what is really going on in a FINCA sub, you need to go to the field and talk to the staff and customers. *La verdad esta en el campo.*

I awake the next day to terrible news from Kansas City. Caesar's wife has a brain tumor. When he came home yesterday, she was unable to talk. She's going in for emergency surgery tomorrow. What's going on? Is FINCA cursed?

I have been putting off visiting our head office in Baku, hoping I would have some positive news to share with them after my meetings with the U.S. Embassy and some of our partners like the European Bank for Reconstruction and Development. "The government is talking about the need for reform, but the impression we get is they are still hoping that the price of oil will rebound so they can do nothing and return to Business As Usual."

In the afternoon, I meet with Elchin, a board member of the newly created Financial Markets Supervision Authority, which has taken over responsibility for the Microfinance Sector from the Central Bank. I have decided not to mince words. I tell him that we have a meeting of all our creditors in London next week, and unless I can tell them that the government is going to back off the interest rate caps and take other steps to restore an enabling environment for microfinance, they won't make any new investments, and they will probably yank the ones they have.

"I've come for good news," I tell him. "Otherwise, I've come to say goodbye."

Afterwards, I meet with Fatima, a dynamic woman who runs the Azeri Microfinance Association. Her view is that if all the international microfinance companies like FINCA disappear in Azerbaijan, private individuals with their own capital will move into the void, although not to the same extent as the MFIs, and certainly not in the more remote, impoverished areas.

I ask her if she thinks there is any chance the government will bail out the sector.

She smiles. "We can hope."

We can hope! Fatima's job, like mine, is to be optimistic in times of crisis. And now I must go and address the staff.

Our head office is a modest affair, on the fourth floor of a building in downtown Baku. The top management looks weary, but the younger rank-and-file are surprisingly cheerful. They give me a presentation on their new call room, which is a new technology we are experimenting with to speed up our loan approval process and lower our costs. The phrase "too little, too late" repeats like a mantra in my head. I suck it up and give them a rousing speech to lift their morale. Afterwards, there are selfies with the Big Boss. I always forget what a big deal it is for my 10,000 employees to actually meet Rupert, whom most have only read about or seen in orientation videos. I don't want to believe we are going to give up on Azerbaijan, once our flagship subsidiary. When I told Prince Hal I was going to Azerbaijan to try to pull off one more miracle, he smiled at me, sadly.

"I like miracles, when they happen, but I don't actually believe in them."

Holy shit. Holy fucking shit, it worked! The day after I depart from Baku, Petruchio emails me to tell me that the regulator in Azerbaijan—not the board member I spoke to, but the top dog himself—met with Fatima and told her: "There are no interest rate caps; you can charge what you want."

We defaulted to bold.

Everyone is in a state of happy disbelief. We have a call with the lenders and Rosalind gives them the news. Several of them state that this could change things, and that we should not wind things up too aggressively but position this as a downsizing of the portfolio, with an eye to still make it as a going concern. Some even say that perhaps the lenders need to consider converting some of their debt to equity. Horatio agrees, saying that we should do just enough each month to keep our equity positive.

I am thrilled. We are still a long way from victory, but at least now there is hope of a better result in Azerbaijan. This is an enormous morale boost for our team there. They now need to really hit the collections and try to bring down the Portfolio at Risk, while cautiously making new loans to only our best clients, via the call center. Go Azerbaijan! You can do it, guys!

I stifle the little voice in my head, now less sure of itself, that had posed the question: Too little, too late?

In Islamabad, Pakistan, for the board meeting of FINCA Microfinance Bank, I stay at the Serena Hotel, part of a chain owned by the Aga Khan, Imam of the Ismaili Muslims, who goes by the moniker "The Prophet". The Aga Khan channels an enormous percentage of his personal wealth into charitable activities benefiting the world's poor. One of these is microfinance. The source of his vast wealth ($800 million) is a financial model similar to that of the Mormon Church, taking a 15% "tithe" off the income of his fifteen million followers. In return, members of the sect get a form of cradle-to-grave healthcare, education and retirement through the social enterprises he has set up.

Hmmm. I wonder if FINCA could get away with that? Interestingly, I hear some have referred to FINCA as "a cult". Should I attach a prefix to my name and tithe my 50,000 followers on Twitter? "The Rupert" needs 15% of your pre-tax income. The Rupert accepts Visa, Mastercard, and PayPal.

Part of the Aga Khan's empire is a set of microfinance banks, some in countries that overlap with our own footprint. Rosalind received a feeler from their rep in Afghanistan who wants to talk merger. I need to tell her what I've learned from Perdita, plus research how their other co-investors have done. The last thing we want to do is hook up as a minority investor with someone who takes advantage of what we have built and never pays us a dividend.

Ah, what a world! Trust no one.

Upon arriving at the Serena, we learn they have received intelligence from a "credible source" that we are going to be attacked by the Taliban. A World Bank conference that was scheduled to take place at the Serena has been cancelled. Despite its formidable defenses, the Serena Hotel in Kabul has been breached twice, once when a suicide hit-squad penetrated the three levels of security, went into the spa and murdered a number of foreigners in the middle of their daily workout, and a second time when a trio of young Taliban smuggled .22 parts in the hollowed-out heels of their shoes and shot up a restaurant full of people having dinner, including young children. So why don't we find another place to stay? Mudassar, the CEO of our bank here, says that the security everywhere else is really weak, and the Taliban is probably now in search of a softer target, since their plan has been revealed.

To be safe, I check with Chris, our Security Advisor, who recommends we stay in the high-end hotel but take our meals and meetings in our rooms instead of the common areas where large numbers of people—targets—gather. Sounds sensible. So why don't we do it? It just seems like too much trouble. And, looking at the crowded restaurant, the prospect of an attack seems remote. And we could pursue the "school of fish" tactic. They can't get us all.

At the same time, I know I am taking an unnecessary, foolish risk. This was how Mike Hammer, my former boss in the labor movement, got whacked, eating in a hotel restaurant in El Salvador. Lorraine will not be happy with me. Her last words to me before I travel anywhere are always a quote from a Jamaican friend of ours: "Don't be foolish, Mon."

Our bank in Pakistan is doing really well, on tract to earn close to $4 million this year, *Inshallah*. We will plow about a million of that into an app that our tech partner, FINJA, has developed for us.

Lesson Learned Swag Box No. 28: Avoid the Trapped Equity Trap

When you're having trouble raising growth equity in a network because of faltering performance, you may be tempted to sell down to a minority position to raise the cash you need elsewhere. Understand that once you give up control over management, you will be at the mercy of the majority owner when it comes to pretty much every decision from the overall strategy to the payment of dividends.

If you are going to pursue this "solution" to a short-term liquidity problem, try to ensure that all shareholders are minority shareholders, and no one holds 51% or more of the shares. This way, all decisions will require at least the agreement of two shareholders, ensuring that there is less risk of the equity of the minority shareholders being "trapped" indefinitely.

I say this in full recognition of the fact that this is exactly the position all the FMH minority shareholders find themselves in. To which, verily I would say unto you, "Better them than you."

TOO LITTLE, TOO LATE

Back home, I check in with my contact at the IMF and tell him how things went in Azerbaijan, and our coup in getting the caps lifted. He says when they go back in a week or so they will encourage the Regulator to put that news up on their website so that no one from the Dark Side tries to undo it, making threatening phone calls to our team. He also tells me that financial inclusion and microfinance are now an essential part of the IMF's agenda when they talk to governments.

And now for the shit news. Rosalind has a call with the leader of the Lenders Group, Claudius, in which he tells her that the lenders are now totally aligned around a full wind-up. The option of FINCA Azerbaijan making it as a going concern is officially off the table. We are leaving, in other words. Striking the colors, firing all the staff, closing the doors and going home. After twenty years.

And why has it come to this? Because neither FMH nor the lenders are willing to put in more capital. Even with the recent improvements in the operating environment, the consensus is that it has come too late. The projections show that the return to profitability, with a rebuilding of the equity and prospects for dividends and an eventual exit for the investors, will simply take too long. So much for "patient capital".

To be honest, FINCA is against our minority shareholders putting in more capital, as it would undoubtedly mean diluting us out of majority ownership and control over the holding. We would lose our non-profit status.

Then Claudius drops another grenade: he wants to put a workout CEO into FINCA Azerbaijan, or "a driver", as he calls it. "And if the driver can get the company back to profitability, then he will turn the wheel back over to FINCA management."

Of course he will. After the car is in the ditch with the front stove in.

"Well," says Mercutio, "if that is what they want to do—which I think is very stupid, by the way—then we need to take FINCA's name off it and turn over the keys."

I concur. "That would be a no-win for us. If it turns out to be a disaster, and the lenders don't recover anything, then we will be blamed because it's 'our staff'. We can't take that risk."

Prince Hal disagrees. "I think we should not reject this proposal out of hand."

The call concludes with no consensus on this point.

I depart for London, for three days crammed with PR and fundraising meetings, followed by two days with the Restructuring Group and then, on Friday, a full day with the lenders.

Oh, and my pal Lear will be there, Rosalind tells me. Lear is the chair of a big fund that is invested in Azerbaijan and several other FINCA subs, like Armenia. He's trying to block all the loan rollovers in all the FINCA subs.

"Prince Hal told me Lear thinks you and I are sleeping together. And that you and Sandra (my former deputy) had an affair."

"Really? Did we? I think I would have remembered that."

"He hates you so much," Roz marvels.

"Do you mind if I punch him in the nose in London?"

"Yes."

This meeting in London is going to be critical. We need two things. The lenders need to sign a "Forbearance Agreement" to protect our management in Azerbaijan while we partially repay some of their loans, about $20 million. Then we need to agree on a "wind-up-disguised-as-a-going-concern" plan, in which we walk the tightrope between collecting as much of our loans as possible while not telegraphing the news we are leaving and have our clients stop paying. Not easy.

And we need to deal with Claudius's proposal. Rosalind thinks he "has a point" in that our team may not be up to managing the wind-down. Too close to it, and all that. Hearts not in it. This is true.

So what the fuck do we do?

"We'll think of something by next Friday," says Rosalind, sounding confident.

We meet with the lenders in a large room in the offices of our London legal advisor. Across the street is a small, narrow park featuring the partially excavated ruins of the Roman wall which once surrounded London. The morning session is testy. A number of the lender reps rise and hurl spears at us, all of which miss their mark, clattering harmlessly on the podium. Lear, as before, issues an appeal for my resignation. We have grown accustomed to this, and none of it prevents us from getting our "asks" out. In the afternoon, the adversaries adjourn to our corners, separate breakout rooms. Rosalind and Prince Hal head out for a smoke. I take a stroll along the remains of the Roman wall. I imagine my ancestors, lifting the heavy stones and fitting them into place. Then, their toil finished for the day, heading off to a mead hall for a jar of ale. Save for putting deals instead of stones into place, for the working stiff, little has changed.

"The jury is back. They've reached a verdict."

We file back into the conference room to receive our sentence. The majority have agreed on the outlines of a deal where we do a "Scale Down" of the loan portfolio in Azerbaijan, in return for the "Forbearance Agreement". There are still a few holdouts who make their displeasure known one last time. The rep from one of our smaller lenders, who has been consistently rude throughout the day, rises, looking straight at me. Here it comes.

"Rupert, you haven't said anything all day. Are you involved at all in this? I mean, why are you even here?"

An embarrassed silence falls across the room. I have anticipated this moment. Before I can speak, Prince Hal comes to my rescue.

"Why do you want him to speak now when you have been saying for the past year that he should shut up and say nothing?"

I raise my hand, to signal Prince Hal that "I've got this".

"Actually, I have been very involved in this process, although mostly behind the scenes. But let me say that I fully understand all the frustration, the disappointment and, yes, the anger that you all feel. And lest we forget, behind each of you are thousands of small investors who are very disappointed, and will lose some or all of their money. We at FINCA share this frustration and disappointment. My team has been working tirelessly for the past year to bring about the best possible outcome to this very bad situation. But let's not forget that for two decades, we all made a lot of money in Azerbaijan. Let's remember that over the past two decades we built a beautiful program in Azerbaijan, which was brilliantly managed by the Azerbaijan team, and which brought enormous benefits to millions of Azeris in every corner of the country. Today, we are taking the decision to dismantle that company. That is a tragedy. Perhaps an unavoidable tragedy. If that is the case, we can only hope that some of the good we did, improving these people's lives, will endure after we are all gone."

Afterwards, we repair to the Savoy, where John, our lawyer, is hosting what can't be called a Victory Dinner, but maybe a Celebration of our Survival.

"I was watching that woman from Triodos," Rosalind says. "Her eyes just got bigger and bigger as you were speaking. She couldn't believe what she had set in motion."

"I've never seen a workout where the lenders applauded a speech by the CEO," John adds.

Prince Hal is on his third glass of wine.

"Stupid cow probably needs a good you-know-what."

Lesson Learned Swag Box No. 29: The Enemy of the Enough

A consequence of a crisis is that trust evaporates between all parties, replaced by a generic suspicion that everyone is tending to their own interests if not actively conspiring to do harm to everyone else. A good example is PROPARCO, the French governmental AID Agency, who had the misfortune to disburse a big loan to Azerbaijan—their first to the FINCA family—just days before the government imposed interest caps on microfinance loans, destroying the sector. Nothing will persuade PROPARCO that FINCA did not have advanced knowledge of this. To be fair, they could be forgiven for this suspicion, as their loan was in local currency and a huge boon to FINCA in the months following, as local currency completely evaporated in the Azeri market. Those who had access to it were among the few able to grow their loan book and stand a chance of survival. As it turned out, however, this advantage disappeared with the interest rate caps which rendered all loans unprofitable.

In a crisis where you have many parties to appease, don't strive to win them all over. You can't. Gain the support of the majority, and let them deal with the holdouts. The sight of your face will only infuriate the unmollifiable and sap the energy you need to see the crisis through.

I dream I am in a diminishing group of friends, lamenting the reduction in our ranks, while a sympathetic (for the Devil?) Mick Jagger looks on from his perch on a cushion in an alcove in the wall. I'm not sure what Mick is doing here. It could be as simple as my son, John, asking if I had any Stones on my iPod, as we drove to our golf game on Sunday. I am quite sure I have some, but he can't find any, perhaps because Mick is preparing for his cameo in my dream.

With the lender meeting behind us, we free up space to worry about other things. Next up in the queue is Tajikistan, a small landlocked nation in Central Asia, runner-up for the prize for the worst governance in the world after Turkmenistan, a country ruled by a giant gold horse. The country is rumored to be bankrupt, a fact that the IMF will be announcing any day now, according to my source. This will send the Country Risk indices skyrocketing, prompting all international lenders to cut and run. We have $5 million from Lear's fund up for renewal, and we have tripped every covenant in the loan agreement. Lear is being obstinate again. Prince Hal did an end-run on him to get our loan in Georgia rolled, and this displeased him. We do not have that $5 million unless we start liquidating our loan portfolio, which will put us on a path to oblivion.

And then there is the consultant's report on the restructuring of FMH itself. I got a peek at the draft yesterday. The main recommendation: gut HQ. Devolve all functions except Finance and HR to the subsidiaries. Their reasoning is that the current structure of HQ is a relic of the past and no longer needed as the subsidiaries are capable of performing most of these functions for themselves, and can do it "better and cheaper."

This is fantastic news. It means we have succeeded in building strong institutions in the subsidiaries that can stand on their own. Huzzah! Our work is finished.

Problem is, it's really not. If it were, why are we still experiencing major performance problems? Why are half of our subsidiaries losing money? The consultants say that is because the subsidiaries are bearing the cost of the HQ operation, which pushes them into losses. There is some truth in that. But it's not the whole story. Some subsidiaries are losing money even without the HQ overhead burden, which only about two-thirds of them are actually paying. And there are still subsidiaries, like Mexico, like Uganda, that are poorly managed. How will that get remedied if there is no HQ around to monitor them and make changes to management when necessary?

The consultants' solution is to empower the subsidiary local boards and top management to make all the necessary changes. Mind, we are talking about boards that meet four times a year, and are often populated with people who never set foot in the country in the course of a year. Management will be left on its own for 350 days of the year.

We actually tried this model twenty years ago. We now refer to it as "The Old Paradigm". It resulted in several of our subsidiaries getting hijacked by our management, and others being racked by major frauds. It might work if we were talking about operating in Germany or the United States, which have functioning (more or less) justice systems and Rule of Law, but this is not the case in the countries where we work.

MUTUALLY ASSURED DESTRUCTION

Across the sea, the head of the French Development AID agency, PROPARCO, sits in his office in Paris on the Rue Saint Honore. Before him on his desk is a signed letter to our CEO of FINCA Azerbaijan, informing him that PROPARCO intends to accelerate repayment of its $8,000,000 loan, disbursed just one year ago. If he sends that letter, he sets in motion a chain reaction that brings down not only FINCA Azerbaijan, but the entire FINCA Microfinance Holding Company with its twenty-three subsidiaries.

Efforts of the other sixteen lenders to talk PROPARCO out of this have so far failed. We were very close to an agreement, but now the Frenchies are blowing it up. We trade accusations. Patience and tempers wear thin. Prince Hal shares an email the head of the French negotiating team sent to him:

Dear Prince Hal,

Thank you for your email. I feel obliged to start with a general remark.

I have heard and read from some of the lenders that, for PROPARCO, the destabilization or even destruction of the complete FINCA Microfinance Holding (FMH) would not matter. I also was told that PROPARCO's decision to accelerate was taken out of frustration and is only aiming at "teaching FINCA a lesson".

The above represent very serious accusations and cannot be taken lightly considering the utmost importance of the Microfinance

Sector in PROPARCO's operations and strategy. It is also very insulting towards PROPARCO's staff, mainly those in my team that are very used to these type of situations and know that special operations require a very cool head to achieve the maximum achievable recovery. It is, finally, totally counterproductive and had unfortunately led to a severe loss of trust and confidence on our side into the real motivations and professionalism of some of the parties involved.

Having said that, I feel that with your (and Gloria's) intervention, communication is starting to improve and I have decided to get involved in order to avoid a further deterioration of the situation. Although this comes a bit late, I really wanted to thank you for this.

Coming back to our small situation and how to proceed to quickly allow you to move on, I want to make sure that everyone is aware PROPARCO will not be signing the FBA.

Well, that's clear as mud. My French is not what it was, and even "was" wasn't so hot, but the way I translate this is: "We look forward to meeting with you to see if we can reach some compromise. In the meantime, our fleet of Mirages, loaded with missiles, is on its way to blast you to Kingdom Come."

Full Disclosure: I learn that PROPARCO's position is not as unreasonable as I initially supposed. It turns out that officials in Paris were uncertain as to whether they should disburse their loan back in May of 2015 and sought—and received—a "comfort letter" from FINCA, assuring them that FINCA Azerbaijan had absorbed the shock from the February devaluation and was on the road to recovery. At the time, this was true. In fact, we were so confident of our recovery in Azerbaijan that I paid a visit to PROPARCO in Paris on June 29, 2015, to discuss with them the possibility of their making an equity investment in FMH. Then, in July, the interest rate caps were imposed, killing the profitability of FINCA Azerbaijan and the entire microfinance sector overnight. In December, having depleted nearly all their reserves in a foolish effort to prop up their currency, the Azeri government threw in the towel and let the Manat float, triggering a second, even larger devaluation. The government, helpful as always, put out a message in the local paper suggesting that microfinance clients should "negotiate" with the banks to obtain more favorable repayment terms, especially on dollar loans. Default rates skyrocketed.

PROPARCO's read is that FINCA should have anticipated all this and declined the loan. Our comfort letter, while not legally binding, burns like a tungsten arc lamp in their hands, incontrovertible evidence of our duplicity. There is no persuading them otherwise.

Into this crisis, Prince Hal dons his cape and flies to the rescue. He warns PROPARCO that if they accelerate, they will earn the undying wrath of the other sixteen lenders, all of whom have long memories. When it comes to doing syndicated deals in the future, PROPARCO will be dead to us, he warns them. PROPARCO's negotiating team tells Prince Hal, sorry, they have a new CEO and he is a stubborn son-of-a-bitch who won't back down. It is a matter of principle, he says.

Principle? The rest of the lending group explodes with rage. What about the "principle" of our $100 million? If PROPARCO accelerates, FINCA Azerbaijan will have no choice but to immediately file for bankruptcy. If we file in Azerbaijan, the regulator will intervene and take over the company. All or most of that $100 million will disappear into the ghostly hands of an army of local lawyers, politicians and Central Bank bureaucrats.

The lawyers go to work. PROPARCO's team tells them their CEO is inclined to take his finger off the red button, but he needs to save face. The climb down takes the form of a side letter which looks remarkably like the Forbearance Agreement the other sixteen lenders will have to sign. Whatevah. Add another 1,000 hours of legal billings.

Meanwhile, back in Washington, D.C., we gather for our FMH board meeting, which comes two weeks before our shareholder meeting in Brussels. Brussels? Two months ago, three ISIS-inspired terrorists set off suitcase bombs at the airport, killing themselves and thirty-two innocent passengers. The Belgian security forces had the info on the impending attack but they sent the warning to the wrong email address. Guys! Better wear our Kevlar.

We have dinner with the FMH board the night before. Iago is my friend again, patting me on the arm and telling me Belgian jokes. He calls Belgium "a failed state with great food". *Sproing.* Prince Hal predicts the two Forbearance Agreements could be signed before the end of this week, at which point we will have thirty days to hammer out a restructuring agreement which, everyone anticipates, will be even more difficult to negotiate than the FBA. It's going to be a long, hot summer. We all drink too much and stagger out to our taxis.

As usual, the most interesting part of the board meeting takes place in the Executive Session, without management. Budgeted in the agenda for twenty minutes, it lasts for over an hour. Mercutio fills me in afterwards.

"We had a huge battle over appointing Rosalind to the board," he tells me, grinning. Unlike most people, Mercutio loves conflict. After the past year and a half, I think I have come to embrace it as well.

"I told them that we were going to keep all of our existing five board members, and proposed that Rosalind take the independent seat. They went berserk. Prince Hal said the minority shareholders would never accept this. He says that Caesar or you need to step down and Rosalind take one of the FINCA positions. I told him this would put her in a terrible position as she would be the swing vote and under incredible pressure between FINCA and the minority shareholders every time there is a disagreement."

"And where was Iago on this?"

"He was the one pushing the hardest for you or Caesar to step down."

My spidey senses. I should find a way to monetize them.

"Hotspur was outraged. He asked how they could possibly tell FINCA who to put on the board."

"Where was Benvolio?"

"He tried to make peace. But he also defended our position."

"So what are we going to do?"

Mercutio shakes his head. "I don't know."

It does depress me that Prince Hal supports the idea of me being booted off the board. I fully expected that from Iago, but I thought Prince Hal and I had an understanding. But he is desperate to get Rosalind on the board and that clouds his vision when it comes to everything else.

SOME CORNER OF A
FOREIGN FIELD

I arrive in Brussels for the shareholder meeting early Monday morning. We follow a winding route through plywood-covered offices and shops to immigration. The airport is still being repaired after the bombing of three months ago. I spot Osric in the line behind me at Immigration. I know he has seen me but is pretending not to have. I reach over the tape and shake his hand.

"Oh, Rupert, I didn't see you," he lies, reflexively.

I'm sure he's at a different, superior hotel, so I don't bother to ask if he wants to share a cab, but hurry through Immigration and out to the taxi stand.

The next day, we convene at IFC's office in downtown Brussels for the shareholder meeting. FINCA is thinly represented. Mercutio and Hotspur are gallivanting through Europe on holiday. Caesar is pinned down taking care of his wife in the wake of her brain surgery. Benvolio is back in Washington, dealing with a business contretemp. This leaves just me and the management team to face the barbarian horde.

As the sole available representative of the majority shareholder, I am asked to participate in the Executive Session. We slip into the usual circular argument over whether FINCA will agree to be diluted so the shareholders can put in more capital.

"If the majority shareholder can't put in additional capital, then FINCA has no choice but to give up control," one of the minority shareholders declares.

I remind him that this not an option; that in order to protect the mission, FINCA can never fall below 51% ownership of FMH.

"Rupert, IFC does not care about your mission," Osric declares. "We need to get FMH back to profitability, and that is our only concern."

Into a horrified silence, two of the other shareholders hastily emphasize that "this is not the case with us".

But Osric cannot pull it back. In a way, it's refreshing. He has said what we all have known, but never articulated. The other investors in FMH, while they may share this view, can never admit it or it will kill their fundraising, which hinges upon their ability to convince their investors that they have a "double bottom line", and a social as well as financial objective.

I propose that we hold a shareholder retreat, to see if we can resolve this impasse that is holding us all, and FMH, back.

"It may be that we can't, and we should just dissolve FMH and go our separate ways. This is fine with me. It's better than just having this same meeting, over and over, like *Groundhog Day*."

After the meeting, Prince Hal claps me on the shoulder, smiling.

"The Peacemaker."

The day dawns gray and drizzly, another weather-led omen of bad tidings. Seems PROPARCO's CEO can't get down from the tree yet. He's demanding a payment before he signs any Forbearance Agreement, even the customized one he insisted on. His lackey is emailing Rosalind, saying: Pay up, now, or the surface-to-air acceleration missile goes out Sunday. Why Sunday, I wonder? Is he saying he fears no one, not even God?

Rosalind is in the UK and not all that available. PROPARCO is trying to pressure her into taking a decision on her own, without consulting the RWG. I wonder how you say "bring it on" in French? *L'amener sur*, says Google. I like the sound of that.

At the RWG, Prince Hal is furious. He calls the PROPARCO negotiator alternately "that SOB" and "that liar". He says the guy tried to blame us for pushing things back to the brink again. Prince Hal will have none of it. He says the Germans and Dutch are freezing their contributions to a number of joint projects with the French Aid Agency, and that if PROPARCO makes good on its threat to accelerate, the consequences will be dire. He says at the end of the call that Pierre "blinked", and said if they receive a request for a waiver before the end of business today, they will "consider" not accelerating. So Prince Hal suggests we do just that: send them a stripped-down Forbearance Agreement in the form of a request for a waiver.

Our lawyer, John, is nervous about that.

"We could be exposing ourselves if certain key protections are not in the waiver."

I concur.

"Whatever we send, we must have the Lender Steering Group sign off on it. The one thing we have going right now is that we are all united against PROPARCO. If the thing falls apart, everyone will look to blame the softest target, which is usually us."

This whole affair seems to have unearthed some ancient intra-European animosities. I never realized the Frenchies could be so duplicitous. In his six-volume history of WWII, Churchill recounted how dealing with De Gaulle nearly drove him mad.

Whoever said banking was boring?

Lesson Learned Swag Box No. 30: Be the Biggest Asshole in the Room

The Argentine Default is a good example of a workout where the holdouts, who comprised 7% of the creditors, ultimately received 100% repayment, while the other 93% took a 70% "haircut". To succeed at this strategy requires patience, and also a willingness to be perceived by the rest of the group as selfish, unreasonable assholes. The Argentinian creditors waited eight years for their payday.

WE BRAKE FOR ELVES

I dream I am at a garden party in my backyard. It can't be in the present, because we are all young, in our 30s and 40s. Parents arrive with their children in tow, so it must be someone's birthday. One mother arrives and starts making out with me. I mean, really putting the make on me, right in front of my wife. Wow! If you are unfaithful in a dream, does that count? Time passes. My backyard has expanded into a broad green pasture, like the ones we saw yesterday when we were out touring the Icelandic countryside. The parents and their children are scattered over the landscape, some on distant hilltops. I catch up with the woman who came onto me and whisper to her that if she is still interested in getting together, I will give her my phone number. I ask her what her son's name is, and she says, "You know already. It's Algernon. And I already have your number."

The Frenchies are at it again. Today is the day they threatened to send off their acceleration letter, which we pre-empted by sending them a draft of a request that they stand down. There is a call planned between the lawyers for tomorrow. The French have made it plain they don't want any of the other lenders on the call; this is a matter between PROPARCO and FMH. We have made it plain that this is an "inter-creditor" matter, and the other lenders will have to sign off on whatever we agree. Which, of course, will be impossible, since we will not agree. Kate is talking to a crisis management communications firm in case this whole thing blows up and we have to get out ahead of it with our version of what went wrong first.

We've come to Iceland at the suggestion of our Canadian friends, Mike and Jacqui, who both serve on the board of FINCA Canada. Iceland is a geological work in progress, a mere twenty million years old, the land scarred by recent lava flows and rugged mountains just beginning to submit to the eroding forces of relentless rain, snow and ice. In the valleys between the mountain ranges lie rich verdant grasslands sluiced by crystal-clear streams fed by the melting snow. The people are unique as well. Initially guileless and diffident, they warm under questioning and reveal a national pride wounded by their recent brush with bankruptcy. There is a lesson for FINCA in the speed of their reputational recovery. Just seven years ago they were loathed by their depositors and creditors. Back then, many people lost their entire savings, seduced as they were by the high interest rates on deposits. Today, everyone wants to go to Iceland, and the tourism boom is healing their financial wounds.

How did they manage it? In part by bringing those responsible to account, and swiftly. They also endured years of penury under a tough austerity plan. Although most of the rogue bankers have since quietly left prison, they wear the virtual shackles of their villainy still and are rarely seen in public. When they do appear, they bake like scones under a heat lamp in the collective glare of their fellow Icelanders.

On our last night in the country, we are invited to the home of an Icelandic family, friends of the Canadian couple with whom we are traveling. Mike, probably the most curious non-child I have ever known, has somehow picked up on Google that some Icelanders claim to have seen elves. Our host, a retired software engineer who had managed to lose only 50% of his wealth in the crisis, tells us of a company that, in clearing ground for a new office building, spared a volcanic formation purported to be a kind of elf condo.

"We don't laugh at people who believe in elves," our host explains. "I personally don't believe in them, and most Icelanders don't, but we respect those who do."

Bad news from Washington. The El Salvador transaction is gummed up. We had hoped to have our first sale concluded by the shareholder meeting, but it's not going to happen, owing to our failure to resolve an outstanding issue with one of our donors. Some donors, including one that gave us a big grant for El Salvador, put strings on their donations, requiring us to keep all the money in the beneficiary country in perpetuity. This does not play well with a transaction that involves selling our assets and taking the proceeds to reinvest in some other country. We thought we had engineered a workaround, but no, one of our team pushed too fast and didn't cover all the bases and now we have a mess on our hands. I am supposed to go down tomorrow to bless the transaction, and reassure the staff of FINCA El Salvador that life will be good under their new employer, one of our competitors. Portia, in an abundance of optimism, has already sent an email to our shareholders, requesting their approval for the transaction. Unless my team comes up with some brilliant solution, we are going to look like total fools.

Just another dose of arsenic into an already toxic, combustible *moule-aux-brussel* for the shareholder meeting, when they come to town the week after next.

My real worry is "the Rosalind Factor", and how we are going to deal with the battle over the FMH board composition. It troubles me that I have not heard from Mercutio. He was to call me after he talked to Hotspur, who had contacted him saying he had talked to Iago on this point and felt "we had reached a compromise". And what "compromise" was that?

"Caesar will resign and remain on the board as a Board Member Emeritus," Mercutio tells me. "He can be an observer but with no vote, and we can appoint whomever we want to take his place. I told Hotspur, no, that's not what they want. He doesn't believe me."

"You're right, that's not what they want. But this is how Iago operates. He will now go to the shareholders and tell them: 'I've got FINCA to where they will accept Caesar stepping off the board. Now you all just need to push to have them appoint Rosalind to that position.' It's so fucking obvious. And I gotta say, bro, it really worries me that Hotspur doesn't see that."

"Rupert, I promise you, when it comes down to it, we can count on Hotspur's vote."

"Just as long as you are the one telling him *how* to vote."

It worries me that Mercutio has not called. Is Hotspur off the grid, camping somewhere? Unlike Mercutio, he hasn't responded to any emails, which suggests that, yes, he's with his son on some mosquito-infested mountaintop, making up for all those years he was never around, and was building the family fortune.

Was that the way to do it? Maybe I was wrong to take this path, to devote my life to helping the downtrodden, to build up a billion-dollar empire in which I have not one *centavo* of equity. When I die, I shall be laid to rest in a pauper's grave, stitched up in a cloth sack like Mozart, shovel of lime to follow. Keeps the rats away. For a day, at least.

I should have been a pair of paws, muffling the roars of silent fleas.

At some point, someone—probably me—needs to clue Rosalind in to the strategy. Preferably before Iago or Prince Hal does, with their spin on it: "FINCA doesn't trust you. They don't want to appoint you as one of their board members." Not the message we want. The truth is, we can't put her in the position of being the swing vote between the FINCA board members and the minority shareholders.

Lesson Learned Swag Box No. 31: Play the Fool

My lifelong friend and *consigliere*, Chema, a Salvadoran lawyer who lived through the civil war with me, told me that the mistake most people make when dealing with their adversaries is to let them know you know exactly what they are up to. "I do the opposite," Chema advised me. "*Me hago el pendejo*, meaning: 'I play the fool.'" If you don't do this, if you yield to the temptation to show your enemy how smart you are and that you see through them, then you will ensure he immediately adjusts his plans to fuck you in a different way. On the other hand, if you keep him guessing, he will stick to the wrong plan and give you more time to develop your counter strategy. And even when he comes to the realization that you know what he is up to, he will never be 100% sure—unless you are dumb enough to tell him.

This, of course, runs counter to all the bullshit that your adversary will tell you about the need to "build trust by being transparent", which is what he wants you to do, and which he will never do.

CLOUDBURST

We are close to obtaining signatures of the lenders to the Forbearance Agreement and the Frenchies on their own waiver. They will also be allowed to receive some of their payment as interest, allowing them to believe that, as we approach the end game, they will—Ha! Ha!—be owed more principal than anyone else, even though they won't actually receive any more total pro rata cash than the other sixteen lenders. In fact, as our lawyer, John, points out, the only real difference is they will pay taxes on the portion of the payment they want designated as interest.

I have a brief email exchange with Prince Hal, who suggests that by signing the comfort letter back in May of 2015, our lenders, especially PROPARCO, may be justified in their view that FMH "mismanaged the situation". He points out that at the time in question "Rupert was the sole CEO". *Sproing*. Where is he going with this? Do I have to push my Prince Hal piece back onto the other side of the chess board?

In the reflection time afforded me during my sojourn in the Land of the Midnight Elves, I took the trouble to investigate how this infamous comfort letter came to be, and my role in it, if any. I am pleasantly surprised to hear from Polonius that it was actually the initiative of Steve, my former CFO, and that the document bears Polonius's signature. I must have been travelling and unavailable. Of course, had I been available, there is no doubt I would have signed it, which I make plain to Prince Hal, just to be clear I am not throwing Steve and Polonius under the bus. Prince Hal issues a swift apology, but urges that we continue to be sensitive to PROPARCO's hurt feelings. I concur, but remind him that if we are too responsive to this "FINCA screwed us" narrative, this is as much as admitting we are in the wrong, and they will persist in their efforts to receive special treatment.

Meanwhile, life goes on. Or, more accurately, death and illness. Lorraine receives the news that her dear lifelong friend, Anita, has passed away, after a lifetime struggle with MS. This is the second close friend Lorraine has lost to that terrifying, incurable disease. Rosalind tells me that her father has been hospitalized after being unable to get out of bed this morning.

I am only twenty-four hours in El Salvador when more terrible news arrives, this time from Santa Fe. My co-founder Juanito's wife is in the hospital with two brain tumors. One has been removed, leaving her partially paralyzed and unable to speak. They will take on the second, larger one after she has recovered from the first surgery.

What the hell is going on here?

The negotiation in El Salvador, which I have anticipated will go smoothly, soon founders. Portia has been wrangling with Gustavo's investment banker all week, and tempers and nerves are fraying. I thought everything would have been settled by now, and that I was just coming down to ink the deal, but Portia tells me this is not the case.

"Gustavo's investment banker has raised new issues at the last moment. He wants us to guarantee a bunch of loans that seem to have issues with their collateral."

"Not going to happen. We're doing this to reduce the liability side of our balance sheet, not add to it."

Yet I suspect Optima is not totally wrong to raise this issue. We have had problems with our collateral here in the past. It often turns out that a piece of land, or a house, has more than one owner. Chema, my lawyer, once said for all the land titles in El Salvador to be valid, the country would have to be ten stories high.

The negotiation continues throughout the day and into the night. At one point, I storm out of the conference room, and Gustavo has to physically block me from leaving the building. It is a far more complicated transaction that it originally appeared, with all sorts of quid pro quos, each of which we fight over like minnows contending for crumbs dropped into an aquarium. Each time we think we have a deal, Gustavo's banker introduces a new demand. Finally, I have had enough.

"Fuck this bullshit! Let's go. Everyone on my team, pack up. We are out of here!"

After my outburst, the Optima team makes a strategic retreat to their breakout room to reconsider their last demand. Suddenly, there is a flash of lightning outside, followed by a roll of thunder. The lights in the office go out. Rain beats against the darkened windows.

"Wow, talk about a bad omen! I guess this deal ain't gonna close."

In the bathroom, as if by way of confirmation, I have another bloody urination.

Early the following morning, Elmer, the FINCA El Salvador driver, drives me down from the *altiplano* and onto the flatland of the Pacific Coast, headed to the airport. A lugubrious rain is falling. We inked the final deal shortly after midnight. I realize I may be leaving El Salvador for the last time.

It was after I had addressed the staff, told them everything would be fine, this was a good outcome for them, etc., etc., that one of them came up to me and said: "It's going to be difficult not working for FINCA anymore. Not waking up every morning and putting on the FINCA El Salvador *camiseta* that I have worn with such pride all these years."

I went to El Salvador for the first time in 1980, not realizing how much of my personal history would take place there. As a Program Officer working for the AFL-CIO's Latin America program, my job description read that I was there to help the *campesinos* set up agricultural cooperatives, similar to the work I did in the Peace Corps in the early '70s. In reality, I had been recruited to the Last Act of the Cold War, organizing democratic unions so that the poor and downtrodden wouldn't join the Cuba-funded communist guerrillas. I went to a retreat in an abandoned monastery, appropriately named *El Retiro,* where I met Rodolfo Viera and the other leaders of *La Unión Comunal Salvadoreña,* a peasant farmer union in the dangerous business of fighting for land reform against one of the most determined and murderous oligarchies in Latin America.

Every one of the union leaders I met that day is dead now. Most died in the civil war, murdered by Death Squads. Dragged from their homes in front of their wives and children, taken for a ride in an armored Cherokee outfitted with electrical wires and alligator clips to be attached to the lips, nipples and genitals, tortured for a few hours for what names they could provide and then shot in the back of the head and dropped in the local garbage dump. Rodolfo Viera, their leader, was murdered by a hit squad along with my boss, Mike Hammer, and a young Seattle lawyer about my age, Mark Pearlman, as they ate dinner in a private dining room at the Sheraton Hotel. Samuel Maldonado, who took over for Viera, survived the war only to drown in a riptide while swimming off the Pacific Coast. Arturo "Chele" Magana was the sole survivor of a midnight massacre on his cooperative farm in Santa Ana. As the army lined his comrades up in their pajamas to be shot, Chele escaped by running barefoot through a cactus field.

Tears sting my eyes as the memory-soaked, tropical landscape races by. I love this country. I love the people. I became a leader here, forged in the kiln of adversity. I learned the hard art of politics, and how to defend myself from those bent on destroying me.

Selling FINCA El Salvador to Optima was the right thing to do. It is the best thing for our clients and employees. But it should have been FINCA acquiring Optima, and not the other way around. We failed our employees. We failed our clients.

With dull surprise, I realize my minority shareholders and board members are correct in pointing out that we have become overextended. I went out to conquer the world, and in doing so made the mistake all empires make: we took on more than we could manage. As we soldiered out to conquer Africa, Eurasia, South Asia and the Middle East, we neglected Latin America. But who could resist the siren call of working in the former Soviet bloc countries, with their beautiful women, their vodka and their dramatic, unfamiliar landscapes? We were there to free them of the shackles of communism, to be part of their movement to democracy and a market economy.

We tolerated weak management in Latin America for over a decade. The competition overtook us, and our ranking in each of the markets fell from first to fifth and eventually to tenth or lower. By the time we woke up, it was too late. From a virtuous circle where growth attracted new capital and talent, we slipped into a death spiral where we lost first money, then employees, and finally clients. In El Salvador, in the early '90s, we had 30,000 clients, which made us the largest microfinance company not just in El Salvador but in all of Latin America. Today, I leave behind a company with just 7,500 clients.

Lesson Learned Swag Box No. 32: When to Break Out of Character

No leader should get angry, shout and scream, or terrorize his employees. But there are times to get angry, and when you do people will be so surprised they will pay attention. And at the negotiating table, it may work.

FOUR BARE ANTS

I am in my car, parked on M Street in front of our office. I am trying to drive away, but can't seem to find first gear. Then I find first gear, but no matter how hard I step on the gas, the car won't move. I realize I have the emergency brake on. I release it. Put it in gear. Step on the gas. Nothing.

Change du scene. I am out of the car, watching my deceased Corgi, Sheila, chasing a cat. The cat shoots into the shrubbery, and Sheila follows. Seconds later, the cat emerges, runs across Massachusetts Avenue, dodging the cars; other times, the cars dodging the cat. Sheila runs after the cat. I cringe as a speeding car narrowly misses her. I run after Sheila, crossing Massachusetts Avenue, but she has disappeared.

I give up. After all, Sheila died ten years ago. Maybe it wasn't Sheila. Maybe this is a dream. I cross Massachusetts Avenue again, not waiting for the "walk" signal. I dodge one car, then another, coming in the opposite direction. Just then, a blue BMW, which is what I drive, comes careening around the corner of 15th and Massachusetts. The driver swerves, not to miss me, but to hit me. I leap out of the way just in time. He glares at me through the driver's side window as he speeds past.

I go to where my car is parked. Or used to be parked. My car has been stolen. Along with my laptop. Along with my wallet. And my mobile phone.

I cross M Street and start looking for a store or a business, somewhere I can borrow someone's cell phone. This is a really long dream. I descend a flight of steps to a store that sells electronics. Inside, several young men are listening to another young man talking about how he starred in a movie about extra-terrestrials. I get their attention. I explain my situation, ask if I can borrow a phone. One of them produces a Nokia and dials 911. He hands it to me. The connection is poor. The 911 operator has someone else on the line. They are discussing recipes.

Change du scene. This is a really, really long dream. I am back on M Street again, holding an armful of dirty laundry. A man, European, walks up to me. Maybe he wants to help me do my laundry. He says, in a stern voice, "You should resign."

At the end of June, Rosalind signs the Forbearance Agreement, along with sixteen of the lenders to Azerbaijan. The Frenchies sign their customized waiver, although not without some last-minute drama. This gives us until August 15 to negotiate a restructuring agreement. Well done, Rosalind.

A terrorist attack in Dhaka, Bangladesh, snatches the headlines away from an attack on the airport in Istanbul just a week earlier, when I was in Brussels. The terrorists seem to be on a tight schedule, mounting an attack a week. In a restaurant in Dhaka, six terrorists hacked a dozen people to death with swords. One of the victims was a young Indian woman just nineteen years old, a sophomore at Berkeley. Shameran, the CEO of BRAC Microfinance and a member of our CEO group, tells us he has been to that restaurant often. "The message is that any one of us could be killed anywhere, at any time," he writes in his email. "We need to live every day as if it were our last."

A soft "click" as another worry bead, Tajikistan, dislodges Azerbaijan and slips into place. Tajikistan is heavily dependent (49% of GDP) on remittances from Russia, whose economy has tanked recently due to collapsing oil prices and sanctions slapped on Putin for invading Crimea. Compared to 2014, remittances are down 65% in 2016. Everyone in Tajikistan is starving to death, in other words. The government holds an urgent referendum to make President Rahmon president-for-life, because he's doing such a smashing job. Then, because the government is running out of money, it increases taxes and fines on the small part of the private sector that Rahmon's family does not control.

We need to get out of Tajikistan. We are losing over $100,000 a month, and our delinquent loans are rising. Rosalind and Prince Hal have been laboring to cobble together a deal with our lenders, similar to what we have in Ecuador, to roll their loans to give us more time to engineer a sale like we did in El Salvador. IFC is not cooperating. They want to force an early wind-up and use the proceeds to offset a $750,000 loan which falls due in September and March.

Terrible news today, this time from France. Eighty-five people mowed down by a murderous Tunisian driving a truck on the seaside promenade in Nice. Has this world gone completely mad?

In New York, I meet with the Microfinance CEO Working Group, the association we created in 2011 to deal with common issues we face like regulation and client protection. Afterwards, over drinks, my friend Scott Brown, CEO of Vision Fund, quizzes me on what I want to do post-retirement. I have told him many times that I am not retiring, but simply stepping back from the CEO role in FMH. He persists. I realize, finally, he is not quizzing me, but himself. Scott is planning to leave Vision Fund, he has his successors lined up, and he's thinking about his next move.

RATS AND LOBSTERS AND CRABS, OH MY!

I dream that I am in a garbage dump, surrounded by rats in various stages of decay. Other rats feed upon the carcasses. One very tiny, tiny rat is barely visible at the bottom of a button-size hole in the skin of large dead rat, gnawing away towards the other side.

Change du scene. Now I am sitting on the front steps of my house, with a bucket of live Dungeness crabs and Guernsey lobsters. The crabs and lobsters are fighting and the crabs are losing. As I watch, a large red lobster snaps a crab in two with its immense fighting claw. The fact that the lobsters are red and not black-green as in their pre-cooked state makes me wonder if they are zombie lobsters. As if reading me telepathically, the lobster that has disposed of the crab turns his stalk-mounted eyes upon me and raises both claws, a signal he is about to attack. I run back across the street to the rat dump.

I am in Guernsey (for real, not dreaming), one of the Channel Islands. Guernsey is a kind of island prison where the inmates are all billionaires. They are prisoners of their own money, which they are terrified will be taxed away by their revenue-starved homeland governments. The residents of Guernsey have to spend a fixed number of days here or they lose their tax status. Seeing the place, you think, "Hell, that's easy." It is charming. It has history, like when the Germans invaded it and took over during WWII. It has eponymous cows.

The denizens are free to roam about its pretty picturesque narrow streets and verdant countryside. It does rain a lot. And it is a prison. A tax prison.

Let me tell you about the mussels. Let me tell you about the lobsters. The mussels are like giant pistachio nuts. They have the same shape, and they yield up the same delicious meat if you are able to crack and pry them open. And, occasionally, one of them is rotten, and you can tell immediately when you have got one of those, and so there is time to spit it back into the bowl. Here the mussels are in a delicious broth of Guernsey cow milk and garlic.

The lobsters are also delicious. Like their cousins from Maine, they have claws. How come lobsters from the Southern Hemisphere don't have claws? I ask my nonplussed waitress this question. She thinks a moment. "Maybe they don't fight"?

PART IV—THE BEGINNING OF THE END

A SUSPICIOUS TRANSACTION

I am in a big house, the contents of which appear to be in a state of either packing up or unpacking. My role in this process is trivial, which makes sense since Lorraine never lets me do anything important when it comes to packing or unpacking. I have been assigned the task of reassembling a piece of junk jewelry, one small step up from a bunch of paperclips linked together in a kind of uber-cheap-looking necklace. The necklace has come undone, and the separate links cut so that in order reconnect them I have to find some small pieces of wire. This does not seem to be a very important task, even for someone as inept at packing as me.

Rocky calls from Ecuador to tell me that Freddie the Tortuga was given the sack today. Funal, the company that tried to buy our bank just a little over a year ago, has folded. Their chair has asked if FINCA wants to buy the parts.

I receive an email from Falstaff, our internal auditor, telling me "we need to talk". When Falstaff wants to talk, it means something bad has happened.

"Where are you?" I ask. Falstaff is the only one at FINCA who travels more than I.

"In Uganda. Remember that office building we built, the one with your graven image on it?"

"It got hit by a meteorite and we have no insurance."

"Close. Anthony, our local head of internal audit, tells me the accountant is having trouble booking the asset."

"Why is he having trouble?"

"He's having trouble because it looks like we paid for the building twice. Once to build it, and then again when we bought the land."

"That was stupid."

"Yeah, and no one caught it. Not Peter, the CEO, not Francis, the CFO, and none of the board members. Not even Philip, the board member who volunteered to handle the transaction for us, brought it to the board's attention."

Now that is suspicious. "So how much are we out?"

"A million."

"Shit. What does Lear say?"

"That is the most unusual part of this deal. Lear defends the price we paid. He says it was worth it."

"What!?"

"That's what he said. But there's more. On the same day of the transaction, the CFO authorized and the CEO signed a check for $200,000 to a company owned by Philip."

$1.2 million and counting.

A day later, Falstaff calls with more bad news.

"Two auditors from the Central Bank showed up at FINCA Uganda this morning. They wanted to see all the papers relating to the transaction. That plus everything else in the internal audit report."

"They knew what they were looking for."

"Exactly. We have a whistleblower."

We call an emergency meeting of the Restructuring Group.

"We need to show decisive action," I tell them. "Otherwise this could go really badly, really fast."

Mercutio agrees. "We need to fire the board member who handled the transaction, and then the management."

"Maybe the whole board has to go?" Prince Hal asks.

"That depends on what they knew and when," Hotspur opines. "It would really help, for starters, if Philip resigned."

Over the weekend, I call Robert, our longest serving local board member and the person I most trust in Uganda. We go back almost twenty years. He's my African Rocky. He agrees to talk Philip into resigning. A few hours later he calls me back and tells me Philip is going to send Lear his resignation letter.

Since Lear hates me, we have agreed that Rosalind will try to persuade him to fire Peter and Francis. I can tell she is nervous about the prospect. I suggest she prevail upon Prince Hal for help. Two days later, she reports back.

"Lear is refusing to change the management. He says we have no proof of any wrongdoing."

Hotspur is outraged.

"The chairman of the board is blocking us? He's putting the entire company in jeopardy!"

"Let me talk to him," says Prince Hal. "He seems to be in denial about this."

Exactly. It reminds me of when we had our big fraud in El Salvador back in '94, my first year as CEO, losing over a million dollars. The program was 100% funded by the Agency for International Development. FINCA was small then, and had AID demanded that we repay them in full, it would have bankrupted us. The local Salvadoran board members went into deep denial and tried to stop me from pursuing the perpetrators. "Rupert, if people find out, we will all lose our reputations," one of them told me. Ultimately, they all resigned, freeing me to chase down and eventually apprehend the authors of the fraud. One of them, the ringleader, had fled to the U.S. We caught up to her in Reno, Nevada, working as a housekeeper. She spent four years in a horrible prison in San Miguel, El Salvador. When she came to trial, her attorney bribed the judge and he let her go.

I worry about Rosalind not being tough enough on the crooks. She seems afraid to offend Lear, because of his control over so many of the funds we rely on. Prince Hal may also be a problem. I do a call with just Mercutio to resolve this dilemma. I think I have the solution.

"Let's kick this over to the FMH Audit Committee. It's logical that the AC should get involved at this point because of the Central Bank audit. Falstaff tells me those audit papers contain detailed findings—if not outright proof—of management's involvement in the suspicious transactions. The Central Bank has got to be waiting to see if we take action. We probably only have a few days, if that, before they intervene."

"There is no question that the AC needs to be informed of this, and immediately," Mercutio agrees. "If Lear won't act, then the AC has to."

There is one other complication. When Mercutio replaced Caesar as chair of FMH, he ceded his position on the AC to Hotspur. There is some question as to whether Hotspur will automatically become chair of the AC, or it will fall to one of the non-FINCA Audit Committee members, namely Prince Hal or the new IFC rep, Hanif. Mercutio thinks we can finesse it so it automatically defaults to Hotspur.

"I'll call Hotspur and tell him I'm going to convene an emergency meeting of the AC, where I will announce that he's the new chair. At the meeting, he has to push hard for action on the CEO and CFO, and then see how Prince Hal and Hanif react. I predict Hanif will be on board with firing them. Prince Hal will have to come along. He can't be the lone holdout."

"And what if Lear defies the AC?"

"I will tell Hotspur to push it, but not so far as to ask for Lear's head. In fact, we can position it to seem that we want to save Lear."

"From himself."

"Exactly."

Oh, what delicious intrigue! Could it be I will have dispensed with two of my adversaries, Freddie and Lear, in the same week?

The Year of the Hyrax.

Falstaff is standing in my doorway, grinning.

"Not again!"

It's Afghanistan, this time. Earlier this year, the Taliban overran the northern town of Mazar-i-Sharif, where we have one of our best-performing branches. Our manager there had the presence of mind to move the contents of the safe to his house, so that when the Taliban blew it open they found only $100. But a few months later, after the Taliban had withdrawn, several of our employees broke bad, robbed us and used the proceeds to emigrate to Western Europe.

"And the damages?"

"$300,000. So far."

Just before the Audit Committee is to meet, Rosalind brings me fresh news. A lifeline is thrown to Lear from an unlikely source: Orsino, our Regional Director for Africa. Orsino has spoken to the CFO of FINCA Uganda, and Francis has convinced Orsino there is nothing fishy about the office building transaction. This is consonant with Lear's position.

"Francis convinced Orsino that, because the seller, a Ugandan woman based in London, technically owned the building that we paid to build, which was going to be leased to us before she offered to sell us the land, that it was entirely legal and logical for her to sell it to us a second time as part of the deal."

"That's pretzel logic. Has Orsino broken free of his moorings?"

"I know, it's crazy. But that's where we are. And Orsino says, 'Good luck trying to fire Peter.'"

Rosalind announces that she is heading off to France for a month, on holiday.

"I don't begrudge you."

"You sound like you begrudge me."

"Stay away from crowds."

"I'll be fine."

"Don't worry, I've got this. Get some rest. Just one favor, before you go."

At my request, Rosalind takes one more run at Orsino. This time, she succeeds. Orsino promises he will convene the FINCA Uganda board on the telephone and tell them they have to sack Peter and Francis immediately, and to hell with what Lear says.

The next day, I get a call from Rosalind.

"Orsino called the board meeting, as planned."

"And? Did he call the question?"

"He did. And, although he and two other board members were in favor of changing out the management, Lear blocked it."

"Why didn't they outvote him?"

"Orsino didn't have the *cojones* to stand up to him."

The AC meets tomorrow. I tell Mercutio I have one more card up my sleeve.

"The board of FINCA Uganda, including Lear, has to be reappointed next month."

"Reappointed by whom?"

"The sole shareholder of FMH. And guess who the sole shareholder rep is?"

"Rupert?"

I have already put Orsino, Mercutio and Hotspur on notice that I cannot reappoint the CFO or the CEO, considering what I know. I related to them Lear's threat when we had breakfast at the Kampala Sheraton.

"He said, 'If Peter goes, I go.'"

Hotspur laughs. "Please don't throw me in that briar patch!"

The Audit Committee convenes in the conference room, with most of the participants remote and calling in. Lear has agreed to be on the phone as well. I am not on the FMH Audit Committee, so I have to rely on sporadic texts from Mercutio to keep me in the loop. Mercutio has told me his plan is to stay silent for most of the meeting, and then, at the end, to say to Lear:

"So you are saying that you knew that we overpaid for the building, and that you are okay with that?"

I tell Mercutio that I spoke to Rosalind earlier this morning, who told me that she and Hotspur spoke last night and agreed to take a middle road.

"The deal is, the CFO has to go, but the CEO can hang around for the time being. They hope that this will be okay with Lear."

"Now that makes absolutely no sense," Mercutio retorts irritably. "Why let Peter hang around? So he can bury any incriminating documents?"

I agree with him 100%. I am also totally ready, as representative of the sole shareholder, to not approve Peter and Lear continuing on the board.

After the AC has started, I get another thought and send Mercutio a text:

Any decision? I am guessing no and Uganda will come off the board agenda since the AC will be split.

Mercutio pings me back:

Still on—totally ridiculous—makes no sense.

A telephonic FMH board meeting has been scheduled immediately following the AC, and we get word that the AC is running over. Must be some hot debate!

Rosalind enters the board call first, sounding weary. Her voice is leached of all the energy she evinced the last time I spoke to her.

The board call goes on for two hours. Lear, stubborn dude that he is, continues to defend having overpaid by $1.3 million for the office and land. He claims that the board was unanimous in supporting this. He claims they were all shown some cost-benefit analysis that demonstrates the deal will be a great hedge against inflation and devaluation of the Ugandan shilling.

"Wouldn't it have been an even better hedge had we only paid the owner what it was worth?" Mercutio asks.

Then it hits me. I recall that when I participated as an observer during the November 2015 board meeting in Kampala, during the inauguration of the new office building, management made the case to spend an extra $1 million to buy the land. I challenged them to increase their profit figure for 2016 by that same amount so that our bottom line wouldn't suffer. Orsino told me later that management had redone their 2016 projections accordingly. So there should be a record of this somewhere, showing that what the board agreed to was not an additional $2.3 million, but only $1 million!

FINCA Uganda's management and our crooked board member, Philip, must have slipped that one past Lear and the rest of the board at some later date, without my or Rosalind's approval. Given the size of the transaction, it should have been escalated to the FMH Management Committee at HQ.

But Mercutio is not done.

"One thing that really worried me was when Lear said that FMH shouldn't object to this transaction as it 'wasn't their money, it was FINCA Uganda's money'. FMH is the 100% shareholder! Of course it's our money!"

Prince Hal mounts a feeble defense of his compatriot, murmuring that he knows Lear well and he could not have meant this.

I have to bite my tongue. Were I to pipe up here, I would say that this is a perfect example of how Lear thinks he doesn't answer to anyone, least of all the shareholders. If the situation were reversed and I were the chair of FINCA Uganda, Lear would be demanding a full investigation and accusing me of fraud.

Alone in my office, I dance a minor jig around the furniture, singing: "Throw ya hands in the ayah, if youse a true playah!"

CLOSING THE RING

This is getting funny! I am in the El Salvador Airport, waiting for a connection to Guatemala. An email arrives from Lear, copying the whole world (well, our world), and expressing his support for our CEO in Tajikistan who has been taking a rash of shit from her lenders over wanting to park some of her dough in our bank in Georgia. Which makes total sense, since the government of Tajikistan, by all accounts, is about to tip over and glom onto any cash they can put their grubby hands on. So get it the fuck out of the country! No-brainer! But some of our lenders, ever distrustful, think we are trying to pull a fast one, and want us to park it in in Germany or Russia, anywhere but in a bank owned by FINCA.

RUSSIA! ARE YOU FUCKING CRAZY, LADY?

Enter Lear, dressed as a modern-day Goethe, coming to our rescue. And I am the *first* person on the list of recipients, as if this were a very intimate communication between the two of us, addressed just to me, the other 1,000 people copied as an afterthought.

Then, like quicksilver on its heels, comes an email from Prince Hal:

Who would have expected THIS two or three months ago?

Well, perhaps I would have, considering that you clearly told Lear that he had to bury the hatchet—and not in my forehead—with Rupert. Because otherwise Rupert had the goods on him, and was building up steam for a major takedown.

I dash off a quick email to Mercutio, forwarding in the whole chain:

Running scared.

The animals returned last night.

I am standing at the picture window in my dacha in the Berkshires, gazing across the savannah at an unlikely congregation of wild beasts. There is an enormous, eleven-foot-tall golden-furred grizzly bear, an antelope, a large, mangy grey wolf, and a lion. I'm quite sure these animals don't belong together. The only time a grizzly and an antelope are paired is when the former is gnawing off the head of the latter. My mien is relaxed as I take this in. Still, habits acquired during my years in war zones compel me to map out a contingency plan for myself, Lorraine and my son, John. This plan involves going up to the second floor, closing the flimsy wooden door behind us and taking up mops and brooms to defend ourselves.

Two problems. First, the grizzly could smash the door to matchwood with one blow of his hairy paw. Second, and more importantly, the dacha has no second floor.

Two days later I arrive in Lahore, Pakistan, for a board meeting of FINCA Microfinance Bank. That evening we gather in the "Haram Room", a windowless converted storage room on the third floor where foreigners can imbibe the local vodka, gin and sorghum beer. Steve, my former CEO and a FINCA Pakistan board member, has brought me a bottle of Wyoming Bourbon. Falstaff excuses himself to take a call from Prince Hal, who is anxious to share some new intel on the situation in Uganda. I suspect Prince Hal thinks he has something that absolves Lear. Sure enough, when Falstaff returns, he looks deflated, as only an internal auditor can whose quarry appears to have eluded him.

"What have you got, Big Guy?"

"Minutes of an Asset Liability Committee Meeting (ALCO) have miraculously appeared, which suggest the board of FINCA

Uganda was fully in the loop on the crooked transaction and approved of it."

I make the eighteen-hour flight back from Pakistan in two chunks, a short one from Lahore to Doha and then the massive haul from Qatar to Dulles. I am sick as a dog, my nose running like the Nile. An astonishing text from Rosalind greets me when I land at Dulles: scans of three letters from the Central Bank of Uganda, one to our board member, Philip, who handled the fraudulent office building transaction, another to our CFO, and the last to our CEO. All three are just one page. The first two are pretty straightforward:

Ya fiyad!

Our CEO gets off with a "strong warning".

Holy shit!

This changes everything. Just as we feared, the Central Bank has acted because we didn't.

The next morning, we have an Audit Committee for Uganda. Rosalind amazes me by starting off with:

"Given that the whole board seems to have had knowledge of this and approved the transaction, management's recommendation is that we dismiss the whole board."

"I would only ask that before we take such action that Falstaff, our internal auditor, completes his investigation," Prince Hal implores.

Hotspur is not having it. "We had this information two weeks ago, we knew the Central Bank had it, and we did nothing because Lear blocked us. If we continue to stall, their next move will be to intervene. We cannot take that chance, gentlemen. As head of the Audit Committee of FMH, I will not take that chance."

"I agree," says Hanif, our IFC-appointed board member. "We have enough information already to take action. Whether the board was involved in something nefarious or was simply incompetent, in either case they all have to go."

We discuss how to communicate our decision to the Central Bank. We agree that it has to be in person. Hotspur says that, unfortunately, he can't travel.

"Rupert, would you be the one to head this delegation?" Mercutio asks.

"I think you, as chair of FMH, should also go."

Looks like I'm getting right back on a plane, headed east. Sick and jetlagged as I am, I feel jacked on adrenalin. We're moving towards the end game and can't afford to make a wrong move. It means I will not be going to London with Lorraine on Monday, as we had planned. My schedule, which includes lunch with a Lord and Lady at the Ivy Club and a live interview on the BBC, will have to be shifted. Lorraine is not pleased. She assumes this is also going to screw up the holiday we had planned in the Lake County with Michelle and her boyfriend. I promise her I will be back in time for that. Back to London, that is.

Later in the day, Rosalind, still on holiday in France, calls to tell me that she spoke to Orsino just a moment ago and he is talking about resigning.

"You've got to talk him down," she pleads. "If we lose Orsino, we lose Africa!"

"Call him back. Get him on a three-way."

Orsino is inconsolable. "This is the end of my career!" he moans. "How will the rest of the Central Banks react when they hear I've been kicked off the board of Uganda? I need to resign, now, immediately!"

"Easy, Big Mon. Trust me, we'll handle it in such a way you come out unscathed. Look, you didn't do anything crooked, right? Lear threw you guys under the bus. He claims you all knew we were overpaying for the office building but approved it anyway. And now we know that Philip made at least $200,000 on the deal. We have to put Falstaff on it. Find out if anyone else whet his beak."

Although it's difficult, I have to determine whether Orsino actually knew, as Lear claims, that we would be paying for the office building twice, and still decided to go ahead with the transaction. As we talk, it becomes clear that Orsino didn't dig into the numbers or review the cost-benefit analysis in any detail. Not a crime, just a cock-up.

"I was distracted," he moans. "I had so much shit going on, and there were so many versions of the analysis that it must have just escaped me! But I promise you, I didn't make a dime off this transaction."

"Easy, Big Mon. No one believes that for a second. But we have to go through the process and subject everyone to the same scrutiny. I promise you, you are going to come out of this fine. You have a long track record of success with FINCA. You've gone to the hellholes of the world, Haiti and Congo, and done stellar work. Me, Mercutio, Hotspur and Caesar, we are going to take care of you, understand?"

As he talks, I can hear him climbing, slowly, down from the ledge.

After I hang up with Orsino, I call Mercutio. I tell him Orsino is off the hook.

"Bro, there is no way we can blow away the whole board, like Rosalind and Prince Hal are thinking."

"I know. But I wasn't going to say that on the phone. So Orsino stays, and I'm guessing Robert and Douglas will tell us the same thing: they didn't realize what they were approving because of the way management presented it."

"Then we're cool. See you in Kampala."

A DISH SERVED COLD

I arrive at Entebbe airport at midday on a Sunday. I have sent several emails to the Central Bank, requesting an urgent meeting, but as yet have received no confirmation.

Relax, Dude. It's the weekend. What did you expect? But if I can't get a meeting early in the week, I may miss my flight to London on Wednesday evening.

Mercutio and Falstaff arrive in Uganda the following day. Mercutio has been installed in the Presidential Suite on the top floor, in recognition of the millions his company spent on hotels during his workout years. It's a good place to set up a War Room. It has a long table in the dining room where Falstaff can spread out all his internal audit reports. We also have a copy of the bylaws of FINCA Uganda and the regulations from the Central Bank governing the composition of the boards in the Ugandan banking system.

Robert arrives around noon. I brief him on the latest developments, and the purpose of our visit, which is to convince the Central Bank that the shareholder, FMH, is going to take action by changing out the management and, if he continues to oppose this, removing the chairman of the board. By now I have confirmation of our meeting at the Central Bank. It's Wednesday at 11 a.m. It's going to be tight making my flight to London.

We spend the afternoon scheming about how to remove the CEO, bloodlessly if possible, and, equally important, whom we will install in the interim. Fortune smiles on us in that we have a good interim in our former CEO from the Democratic Republic of the Congo, who is in Uganda on a short-term assignment. He should be acceptable to the Central Bank. For the longer term, we have a possible candidate in the former CFO of FINCA Uganda who has recently stepped down as CEO of an MFI in Kenya. I make a note to call him and see if he's interested in coming back to FINCA Uganda.

The delicate part of this operation is going to be convincing the Central Bank that we have everything under control and they don't have to take action. Falstaff is concerned that by removing the CEO and CFO, both of whom are on the board of directors, we will fall below the minimum number required by the Central Bank. This will only be a temporary situation, until we find replacements for them and Philip, but if the Central Bank wants to get technical on us, it could be a problem.

"I think they will work with us," says Robert. "They should give us some time to find replacements."

Now we need a good reason to remove the CEO, one that doesn't depend on Falstaff coming up with more evidence of his direct involvement in the fraud. If we make an ironclad case for putting Peter on suspension, we can remove the last impediment to a full house cleaning and install Mario, our former CEO of the Congo, as interim CEO.

"Peter and Francis issued a check for $200,000 to a medical supply company owned by Philip, the board member who handled the office building transaction. That seems like a lot of money for management to distribute on its own authority. What is the maximum permitted under FINCA Uganda's policy?"

Falstaff flips through the FINCA Uganda bylaws. His finger stops mid-page. He looks up, grinning. "Twenty-five thousand."

"Got 'em," says Mercutio. "No way the Central Bank will object to us putting Peter on suspension when we tell them that tidbit."

This is looking better and better.

"There's one other thing." Robert produces a copy of a letter we have not seen, from Lear to Charles, the Director of the Central Bank in charge of supervising the microfinance companies, including FINCA Uganda. Lear is asking for a meeting in early September to "clarify some things". He is also offering to resign, if that is what the Central Bank desires. "How do we handle this one?"

"Let's just play it by ear," says Mercutio. "Maybe it won't come up."

We are fully strapped as we head off to meet with the Central Bank on Wednesday afternoon. We really don't know what to expect. Charles, the head of the non-bank financial institutions division, listens, poker-faced, as Mercutio goes through the introductions. I explain that I founded FINCA Uganda twenty-two years ago along with Daudi Mageriko, a well-known member of President Museveni's cabinet, who at the time was a lowly local politician out in Jinja, a small town at the origin of the Nile. "I had an eye for talent back then," I boast.

Charles thaws a little. "Yes, Daudi said exactly the same thing at the inauguration of your building last year."

I wonder if this is a jab at my having been absent at my own honoring ceremony, where they put up the medallion on the building's entrance.

At this point Mercutio brings up the transaction, and the role of the board and management in it, which Charles and his two subalterns already know from having walked into FINCA Uganda last week and confiscated Falstaff's working papers. What they don't know is how Lear had been blocking the rest of the board—not to mention the shareholder, FMH—from taking action. Their eyes widen as I describe how the Audit Committee of FMH requested the board of FINCA Uganda to put Peter on suspension and Lear refused.

"Yes, we have not been happy with the way decisions are taken at FINCA Uganda," says Charles, frowning. "It seems that only the chairman and the management are involved, and the rest of the board is not consulted. I understand that the chairman is going to resign. We would like to see a resident of Uganda as the new chairman. It makes communication so much easier."

"We will make that happen," Mercutio promises.

Now comes the delicate part. Lear and even our own General Counsel, Polonius, have warned us that if we ask Lear to resign and put Peter on suspension we will be down to only three board members, when the legal minimum is five. I have argued that we have to go for it—default to bold—since there is no other way we can retake control of the institution. But we do need Charles to bless these actions.

"We have a number of candidates for the board," Mercutio says, showing a half dozen resumes he has brought with him. "We are still in the process of vetting them. We want to make very sure we get the right people this time."

The allusion to Philip does not go unnoticed.

"We totally agree to have a resident chairman and 50% Ugandan residents," I add. "Our goal is the same as yours: to have strong governance and strong management. As much as we agree—and are grateful—with the action you took, we are embarrassed that you felt compelled to act. We never want to be in that position again."

Charles nods. "It is important not to rush the process. Find your candidates, vet them, and then we will vet and approve them through our own process."

Falstaff gives me a meaningful look. I nod.

"Sir, I need to ask, just to be sure. Are you saying you are okay with us falling below the regulatory minimum of five board members, temporarily, while we identify and vet new board members?"

"That is correct."

We got it. I risk going one step further.

"I have heard from our team that our relations with the Central Bank of Uganda have not been the best over the years.

We need to change that. I want to say now, from our side, our goal is that of all the financial institutions in Uganda, your best relationship is with FINCA."

I'm referring to an incident where Orsino, our Regional Director for Africa, pissed off the Central Bank by arguing with them over some trivial point in their audit report. You don't fight City Hall. Or in this case, the Bank of Uganda.

"That is our goal as well," says Charles, smiling. Then he produces Lear's letter. "I don't think that I need to have this meeting, now that the chairman will be stepping down, do you?"

It's hard to imagine a better outcome. Now we need to report back to Prince Hal. Back at the War Room atop the Sheraton Kampala, we get Prince Hal on the phone. I detect a note of skepticism in his voice as he asks if the proposal to clean house immediately came from us or from the Central Bank?

"They told us, emphatically, they wanted us to change out the chairman and the CEO, and not wait until we appoint new board members," I tell him.

"Oh, and they don't need to see Lear again," Mercutio adds.

When I arrive in London the following day and open my email, a scan of Lear's resignation letter is in my inbox. We are on a roll. In the past forty-eight hours we have taken full control over FINCA Uganda, officially fired the CFO, received Lear's resignation, put Peter on suspension and installed Mario as interim CEO. I have an exhausting schedule of meetings with potential donors and media interviews ahead of me, after which it's off to the Lake District for a holiday!

During the course of the day, I receive an email from Falstaff with some clips from a Kampala tabloid featuring pictures of Peter and Francis under the headline **GO TO HELL!** But the article makes FMH, the shareholder, look decisive, so we don't demand any retractions. Orsino reports that the staff appears—with few exceptions—pleased with the changes.

In victory, magnanimity. I seek Prince Hal's advice on whether or not to write Lear a brief note, conciliatory in tone, recognizing his great contribution to the microfinance industry over the years—or whether this might be taken as a cynical, empty gesture or even evidence of my gloating over his demise, all of which, to be sure, were phases I had passed through. Prince Hal responds:

Lear doesn't "hate" you for personal reasons, but he considers you as somebody who too late understood that it is time to hand over key operational responsibility to younger and/or more commercially tested people. He fears you are too much "in love with power" to let operational reins go. This is a bit funny though, because when describing you as such, he actually describes himself as well, just like in a mirror. And sometimes he even understands this.

On balance, I have been fortunate in my adversaries. Most are afflicted by a fatal flaw and I have only to wait for it to express itself and then abet their downfall with a gentle push. Such is the case with Lear. He could have easily remained in power for another three years, completing his destruction of FINCA Uganda as I stood by, gnashing my teeth in frustration. His inability to admit he was wrong about his two acolytes became his undoing.

As a denizen of Lear's second box, I had to accept Lear's eternal hatred as a given, Prince Hal advised me, just as I understood he would defend Peter and Francis to the end, despite the mounting evidence that they enabled the fraud. "If Peter goes, I go," Lear threatened during our meeting, over breakfast at the Kampala Sheraton Hotel. I stored those words for another day. That day has come.

**Lesson Learned Swag Box No. 33: Know Thy Enemy
Your adversary may have a weakness that can be used
against him. When you discover it, be patient, and wait for
the right time to take advantage of it.**

A few days before Board Hell Week, out of the blue, an
email from Prince Hal:

*On Tuesday I had figured out that it would make sense for me
to have additional meetings with IFC in D.C. next week on
completely unrelated issues. Shortly after I contacted IFC on
a possible meeting for the 14th, it seems Osric got notice of my
staying on in DC on the 14th and asked me to meet with him
"confidentially" as well.*

*My first reaction was that I felt reminded of that notorious
evening before the April shareholder meeting where a strong
group within the minority shareholders, led by Osric, had before
my arrival to the meeting in closed session argued for, or almost
decided on, an "exchange of management at FMH", in the
sense of an external management team being brought in. I had
violently opposed these plans in the ensuing discussions, and
certainly managed to turn around at least FMO, KfW, Triodos
and Responsibility. Osric then gave up on this that evening.
Maybe I didn't have to turn the others around because they had
been skeptical about Osric's proposal to bring in an external
management anyhow, and just needed someone to reassure them.
Anyhow, management's excellent performance the next day during
the shareholder meeting, in which Rosalind largely presented the
full reform agenda, silenced such ideas. And such ideas didn't
reappear again at the next shareholder meeting in Brussels.*

*Given all what has been achieved since then—wind-down
Azerbaijan, closing up to the split with a slimmed head office,
sale of El Salvador, close to solutions on Ecuador and Tajikistan,*

co-investments in the pipeline, sale of Mexico close by, central lending facility being debated in final phase—I can hardly imagine that even Osric is still driven by such weird ideas of exchanging management with externals, which were driving him back in April.

It might even turn out the opposite, with IFC people suddenly becoming supportive?

Still, I will take that "confidential" meeting with Osric on 14 September, listen to what he is going to say, and of course take my position as violently as in April again if necessary.

So it was not my overactive imagination or paranoia: as I suspected, Lady Macbeth was sacked because she had failed in her mission to take me out, and Osric, a member of IFC's dreaded work out group, her back-up assassin, now carries her remit. Thank God for Prince Hal! When this is all over, I shall confer upon him FINCA's highest honor, the Golden Tree. Touching that Prince Hal sees the day coming when the IFC people will be "supportive". Pigs really can fly, I guess.

Meanwhile, the battlefield has shifted to Tajikistan. Two of our lenders have gone rogue on us and are conditioning any rolling of their loans upon a pledge from FMH to put in unlimited capital to maintain our Capital Adequacy Ratio. Our CAR—the ratio between our capital and assets, the key measure of our solvency—has been gradually deteriorating as our loan book declines under the dual pressure of falling demand and rising provision for bad debts. If we yield to this, it will become the new standard all lenders will apply network-wide. It's the ghost of Azerbaijan, and the pivotal moment when FMH was unable to stand behind one of our subsidiaries and put in more capital, continuing to haunt us.

Yet, through all this, we continue to make progress on other fronts. We are about to undertake a pretty murderous downsizing at headquarters and the regions, which will undoubtedly please our shareholders and lenders. Nothing like a little blood on the floor to bring a smile to the lips of a return-starved investor. Especially a so-called "social investor".

At the holding board meeting, the non-FINCA board members resurrect the fight over board seats. They want us to use one of ours to put Rosalind on the board, replacing one of the current board members, preferably me or Caesar. Mercutio has weakened a bit on this and thinks we could live with Rosalind being the "swing vote".

"We will just replace her if she votes with the minority shareholders on any critical issue," he reasons.

I point out to him that this will mean we lose a great CEO.

"So what's the answer?" Mercutio is clearly frustrated.

"I think we keep our five existing board members, add an 'independent' who is not Rosalind, and put Rosalind on the board but without a vote."

"You think they'll accept that?"

"Hanif will like it. He once said that he thought CEOs should be on boards but without voting rights. And we have the case of Uganda, that so-called model of banking governance, where both the CEO and CFO were on the board, but without votes."

I see Mercutio's eyes light up.

"Are you sure about Uganda?"

"Pretty sure. We wouldn't have been able to remove them if they had a vote, right? Because Lear would have sided with the two of them against the other three and blocked it."

Mercutio asks me to check to be sure. But I've brought him around, I think.

"God, they are just going to *hate* that," he says, smiling in anticipation. I have never known anyone to relish conflict as much as Mercutio.

Azerbaijan, our perpetual migraine, is the last thing that stands between us and profitability. If we can get it off the P&L, we will be profitable again, and our elusive turnaround will be official. But to get it off our balance sheet we would need to persuade the lenders to take it, which they have shown no inclination to do. The Monitor—the same consultants who aided us with our restructuring, and recommended we give up control over our subs—has recommended that we cease lending and turn FAZ into a collection agency. They have put in writing that if we do this, we can collect another $10 million. We think this is mad. One of our competitors tried this and their clients immediately stopped repaying. The Monitor insists this will not happen. No one is still lending in AZ, they say. True enough, but they make no mention of the fact that all the banks who have stopped lending have arrears rates of at least 60% of their loan portfolios. As I tried to warn Rosalind and Horatio, these guys have put us in a no-win box. If we refuse to stop lending, then we will only make our goals, which are $10 million less in collections. If we do it their way and fail, they will claim "FINCA's heart was not in it". Either way, they win, and we lose.

It's looking more and more like the only solution is to "give them the keys". We would be utter fools to continue to manage a wind-up when we believe the approach they are forcing us to take will result in disaster.

I've been battling a mild depression lately. Could be the fact that I am ramping up my Hemochromatosis blood lettings to weekly in an effort to beat my ferritin reading, currently at 280, down to 50. But I know it is also related to my slow-motion withdrawal from the CEO role. As Rosalind has stepped up, I have stepped down.

As Lear observed, the slow leaching of power, akin to the blood being taken out of my body, 500 cc at a shot, is something I feel palpably. Watching Rosalind, Polonius, Horatio and Falstaff working so well as a team—and without me—is painful. And, of course, the fact that it is yet one more flagstone on my gradual march toward oblivion.

With that cheerful thought, I set down my pen for the day.

PART V—THE END OF THE END

I am on some kind of lake, and my son, John, is weeping over a dog that has been attacked by other dogs. The dog's wounds are horrible, and its fur has been gnawed away from the lower part of its body, revealing pink, bleeding, skinless flesh. One of the attacking dogs comes in for another bite. The dog apologizes, but doesn't stop gnawing.

A talking dog?

Having survived Board Hell Week in good form, we now turn immediately to preparing for a meeting with the shareholders in Zurich on the 28th, ten days from now. In this regard, Prince Hal intrigues us with the news that he believes there is a real chance the shareholders will come back to the table now if we present them with a credible business plan. Furthermore, he thinks he knows who needs to lead the charge in this effort:

In order to launch such an inter-shareholder discussion, the minority shareholders need a clearly designated FI shareholder representative, a face with a clear role, as discussion partner. I would strongly propose that Rupert as president of FI should play this role, and actually exclusively plays this role in the SH meeting in two weeks.

I must be dreaming. At any moment, a talking dog will appear and ask me if I want to play fetch with him.

Does this mean that I have made a complete comeback? I think about my pariah status of a year ago, with all the shareholders and minority board members, except Prince Hal, clamoring for my head.

Not so fast there, pardner. We still have hills to climb. Over the weekend, Rosalind calls to tell me that IFC, Responsibility and EBRD in Tajikistan are demanding a commitment from FMH to put in capital "without limitation", whatever is required to maintain FINCA Tajikistan as a going concern.

LET IT BLEED

My dog, Penny, and I are hiking down a rocky path on some mountain, probably in Maine. Implausibly, this little ten-pound mini Dachshund dislodges one of the boulders, causing a mini avalanche. I freeze and cringe as Penny jumps among the cascading boulders, barely avoiding being crushed, and landing, finally, to my great relief, at the bottom of the path. But wait. One of her legs is trapped beneath a gargantuan, unliftable stone. She turns her pleading eyes to me. Oh, look. Now a giant monitor lizard (in Maine?) has emerged from the undergrowth and is advancing on Penny, its pink tongue quivering in anticipation.

It's a sad day at FINCA. We have finally pulled the trigger on a severe downsizing, letting go twenty-two of our employees at HQ and the regions. I hear first from Rosalind:

I want to send this to the board but I'm just sending it to you because I know how bad my heart is bleeding.
   We let countless people go today.
   Good people.
   Smart people.
   Talented people.
   Committed people. People with families. People I count as friends.
   We are lucky. They were gracious and professional and my team worked so hard to make sure the process was fair and respectful.
   I don't ever want to do that again.

I'm done fighting with the shareholders and the lenders and the politics. We have a business to run, and it's exciting and wonderful. And I need your help to get everyone in line to help us focus on that.

If you can't or won't, I understand. But we can't and won't keep putting Humpty-Dumpty together again.

I can see why she doesn't want to send it to the rest of the board.

The next person I hear from is Petrucho, our Regional Director for Eurasia. He has been with us for seventeen years.

Greetings Rupert,

I write to thank you for the great opportunity it has been to work for FINCA.

Today I have personally let go the entire Eurasia Hub team, in keeping with the requirements of the restructuring mandate from FMH.

I have done this believing that the institution can and will benefit from a more demand-driven support structure relative to its subsidiaries.

I will not opine further except to say that I worry about where we go—structurally, culturally, and interpersonally in the future. The FINCA that I came to work for is no more, and I am not sure how long the accommodation can continue.

I am grateful for the huge experience that FINCA has afforded me, and the personal mentoring that YOU have afforded me.

I trust that you will receive this as my personal thanks for at least part of a career well spent.

Wherever it goes, at least wherever I am, the FINCA spirit will be celebrated in drink and song.

For as long as the joint-road continues, let it be with good courage and companionship.

Let's catch up some time.

I picture Petrucho in his flat in Baku, alone with his cats and a large bourbon. His ex-wife is on the other side of the world, in Myanmar. They separated last year. I dash off my reply:

A dark day, my brother, no doubt about it. I have been just stunned at the speed with which so much of what you built has been dismantled, especially Azerbaijan. I know we could have weathered this storm with more cooperation from the government and our "partners", but we have to put that in the sadder but wiser column.

As to the future, it certainly will not look like the past, but I still hope that, after a period of recovery, FINCA will be one of the MFIs still standing and growing again, although probably not in Eurasia as it did in the past. I know it's hard to reflect on the past right now, but you can always be proud of what you and your team built and also how it carried the rest of the network through years of growth and allowed us to absorb the losses from the fuck-ups so those subs could be still standing today. No small accomplishment.

Stick with me, pardner. I think we are slowly but surely emerging from the storm, and the good times will return. And thanks for all the brilliant work you have done and will do in the future. I know you have had some hard personal shit to deal with and I understand that from personal experience. That, too, will be repaired in the fullness of time.

Had another leeching today. I also received my ferritin results, which showed only a two-point decline to 185 from 187. At this rate, it will take me more than a year to get it down to 50. In the meantime, I will continue to stick to lampposts and have my body turn to magnetic north every night.

I am in a giant amphitheater. My FINCA colleagues and I, as well as several other NGOs, are being held captive by an ISIS-like terrorist group. They are forcing us to play a game where the leaders of the NGOs are forced to charge the terrorists. It reminds me of a movie starring Jennifer Lawrence. I watch, riveted, as the first of the leaders trots up the track on the far side of the stadium. He is too far away for me to be certain, but he appears to be unarmed. After he has run about fifty yards, a burst of automatic weapon-fire erupts from the shrubbery on the far side of the stadium. The runner pulls up short, his body shaking like he's doing some awkward dance. He wheels and drops face down on the track.

Change du scene. I am on the side of a two-lane blacktop, watching my three dogs, Fluffy, Penny and Bruno chasing the passing cars. Lorraine calls out to me from the house, asking me where Penny is. I don't want to tell her where Penny is, as I don't want to worry her. I don't know what Bruno is doing there. Our Chihuahua has been deceased for two years now. A lawn repair truck drives by and all three dogs take off in pursuit. The driver takes note, makes a U-turn, trying to shake them off. Now he's driving on the shoulder, heading straight for me. As I watch in amazement, the three dogs upend his pickup, which does a complete flip, landing back on its tires. Now the front end of the truck has become one big lawnmower. The driver accelerates, bringing the whirring blades to within inches of my feet.

Change du scene. Back to the Hunger Games. I realize, as president of FINCA, I must be the one to make the deadly run down the track towards the terrorists concealed in the shrubbery on the far side of the amphitheater. For some reason, I am relaxed and not troubled by this thought. Then I realize why.

This is a dream.

Lesson Learned Swag Box No. 34: The Goodbye Look
Inevitably, in the life cycle of a business, circumstances will require you to downsize to survive. This is not an easy thing, but it is often necessary for the company's survival, when all other remedies have been exhausted. Many of your loyal staff will understand this, but some will not. Don't flinch. But also, do everything you can to make the transition an easier one for the Departed. Make one of your goals be to have them say they were treated fairly. You never know, you may hire them back one day.

AFTERMATH

London, Amsterdam, Zurich, Washington, D.C., Uganda, London, back to Washington, all in the space of ten days. It was productive, all except the meeting in Zurich with the shareholders, which resulted in the usual: nothing. We need capital, they won't provide it unless we turn over control of the holding to them. So we try to raise capital by selling off some of our subsidiaries, and we try to find co-investment capital at the subsidiary level, sidestepping the holding company until it becomes profitable again.

Which is when? At the shareholder meeting, Horatio tells the shareholders that we anticipate a year-end loss of $29 million. Then he tells them: "There will probably be some other hits we take in terms of write-offs which could add to that loss." Their ears perk up. This is one of Horatio's unfortunate habits: when it comes to bad news, he tries to deliver it incrementally, with the result that when the final number comes in and it's much larger than the forecast, we lose credibility with those on the receiving end.

"Horatio, next time just tell them to expect something on the order of $50 million," I implore. "That way, when it hopefully comes in lower, maybe they will be less disappointed."

Poor Rosalind. Poor Prince Hal. They keep hoping, in the face of the mounting, incontrovertible evidence to the contrary, that they can convince the minority shareholders to sign up to another capital raise. I especially feel sorry for Prince Hal, who has worked his ass off, trying to keep his fellow minority shareholders on board.

A cold, drizzling gray autumn day on the rockbound coast of Maine. We usually don't come up this time of year but one of our renters bailed and I was able to squeeze in a few days. Yesterday, Lorraine and I went hiking and came back with some unwelcome hitchhikers: a pair of deer ticks. I thwarted mine scrambling up my left leg, just inches short of my nether region, which I assumed was its objective. Lorraine's had already stuck one of its eight paws into her shoulder, but not yet deep enough to begin sucking. My brother, Dan, tells me we still have to observe the skin around the wound for the next few weeks to see if the telltale red ring appears, signaling a Lyme's Disease infection.

We owed the timely discovery to a pair of anonymous hikers who left a note under my windshield wipers, warning us that they had picked thirty of the little buggers off their clothing and to beware. Where but in Maine would you find someone considerate enough to plant a warning like that on your windshield? What a great state.

Dan tells us our part of Maine is "Tick Central" and that, not only that, but the mosquitos now carry Encephalitis, which kills you in a matter of days. What the fuck is going on in the Bug Kingdom? What did we ever do to you?

The Azerbaijan drama continues to play out. Horatio has come up with an ingenious idea: accept the lenders' condition to stop lending, but with the proviso that they automatically forgive enough of their loans each month to keep us at zero losses. I'm touched he actually believes they will accept this. I think, after eighteen months of this crap, a kind of group hysteria has set in within our team.

I am traversing a barren, dystopian landscape on foot, destination unknown.

Change du scene. Now I am on a high cliff, overlooking a boundless ocean, waves beating on the rocks below. Behind me, on the land side, is an expanse of flat, dark rock, where rainwater has pooled up in the indentations. One puddle has been chiseled out to form a deeper pool, square in shape, and currently hosting a pair of naked women swimmers.

Change du scene. I am climbing up a set of narrow steps, sized to fit the diminutive feet of Aztecs, towards the top of a pyramid. At the summit, I stare out across a verdant plain. At a railway station, a contingent of soccer players, wearing their colored jerseys, is debouching from the railway cars and onto a playing field. Eager to join the game, I begin my descent. But the steps are gone now, replaced by a series of high dolomite columns, increasingly shaky as I extend my foot to test their stability. The near columns are close together, but each successive column is set, diabolically, farther and farther apart, so that to reach them I have to jump. Who do they think I am, Super Mario? I glance behind and see I am not alone: someone is following me. Not with malicious intent, but merely facing the same dilemma as I. Towards the bottom, where the consequences of a fall appear survivable, I find that I must dislodge one of the columns in order to place it midway between my current position and the one I must jump to. But in so doing, I have now left the man descending behind me stranded, without the means to continue.

Change du scene. I am down on the playing field, on the sidelines, watching as sides are chosen. There are two complete teams of eleven, and then a second pair that are short several positions. The short-handed teams, of which mine is one, are told to take the field first. I am in my familiar dream-world dilemma of having no proper equipment. At first, I try on what turns out to be a pair of women's shoes, pinched at the toes and tasseled, with an embroidered design on the sides. Nice but not very practical. Finally, I locate my boat shoes. These will have to do. I take the field, and begin playing—or trying to. I can't reach any of the balls, and no one passes to me. Finally, a ball rolls towards me, right in front of the goal. I take my leg back to strike it, miss, and fall on my ass. One of the players whispers something to me. Looking down, I see that I have been playing with my fly wide open, and my shorts unfastened. The referee calls full time. We leave the field. "Did we win?" I ask one of my teammates. He shakes his head. He doesn't know either.

The Latin America team—what's left of it—meets in Washington this week, while I am up at my cottage in Camden, Maine. I feel guilty, but just as happy to miss what promises to be a gloomy event, attended by the staff who have survived the restructuring bloodletting, which means just the country teams, all of the regional staff having been let go.

Rosalind tells me she is going to have a meeting with Rocky in which she tells him, definitively, that she has no need of his services after January 1. I try to convince her that this a mistake, that Rocky represents the only hope of saving FINCA Guatemala. I confess it was at my urging that she placed my former deputy there, who had asked me to give her a shot at a field position. She isn't cutting it, and I'm imploring her to put Rocky in charge. Rosalind tells me Rocael is simply too difficult for her to manage, and he doesn't "obey my instructions". She's right about this. I don't tell her that is because some of her "instructions" don't make sense. I try to convince her that a person who gets results—as Rocael has unquestionably done in Ecuador—is far preferable to obedient staff who don't. Rosalind flares up. She tells me her staff is great, and has been a huge help to her engineering the sales of El Salvador and Mexico. Now it is my turn to flare up. I tell her that the results and people she values are those who can sell subsidiaries, not those who add value to them.

"When we had a problem with results in Mexico, your response was not to fix it, but sell it. When we had a rogue chairman who was blocking the removal of our underperforming management in Uganda, your answer was to sell it. When you can't find funding for Nigeria, your answer is to sell it. You're running out of world, Rosalind."

By now, both of us are yelling. Rosalind says that if I feel that way, maybe she is the wrong choice to be my successor. I let my silence speak for me.

Later, Rosalind emails me to say that she wants to talk more about all this. I apologize for "going Wasp" on her. We Wasps, for some reason, keep our mouths shut for months and then vent all at once on the things that have been bothering us. This is not Best Practice, the communications majors will tell you. As a Wasp, I say better late than never.

I do worry that maybe Rosalind is the wrong choice as my successor. She does so much so well, but there are some big things we disagree on. I wish she would go to the field more. She seems totally blind, sometimes, to the kind of talent it takes to run a program. It was my fault to push my deputy on her in Guatemala, I admit that. But if Rosalind leaves her in place, having recognized the problem, then it becomes her fault.

DEATH IN THE FAMILY

I have a call I've been putting off, to my co-founder, Juanito. His wife, Mimi, is at Stage Five with her cancer. It's spread throughout her entire body. She's moving into hospice care. Finally, I call Juanito, figuring it will go straight to voicemail, but after three rings he answers.

"How you holding up, *hermano?*"

"Good, good. Hey, thanks for calling." He sounds broken, exhausted. Not like the perpetually upbeat Juanito I know.

"How's Mimi doing?"

"Well." A dry laugh. "As good as can be expected, I guess. She's kind of in and out of consciousness and not really able to communicate. But I know she understands and appreciates having the whole family here and everyone keeping her in their thoughts. You wouldn't believe how many well-wishers have called over the past few days. Muhammad Yunus, Sam Harris; all the gang from the old days."

Sam Harris founded Results, a citizen's lobby that persuaded Congress to appropriate $100 million for microfinance, twenty-five years ago. Juanito first told me about him when I flew out to console him about the death of his younger son, killed in a car accident. Unbelievably, Mimi's son died in similar circumstances several years later. They somehow surmounted these unimaginable tragedies, carrying on with the same unsinkable bonhomie. Mimi bravely fought cancer the first time it struck, over a decade ago, eschewing chemotherapy in favor of a homeopathic cure. To everyone's surprise—except Juanito and Mimi's—it worked, and the cancer went into remission. It was their trust in the natural path and strong faith in each other that carried the day.

Mimi passed away on October 31. I got the news on Facebook two days later, reading a post from Sam Harris. I was in Kansas City on November 1 and when I asked Caesar how she was doing, he said, "She's not going to make it." I guess John was too overwhelmed to even call his older brother with the news. I tried to reach him but had to leave a voicemail.

VOTAGEDDON

I am in my cookie-cutter home in Levittown, Long Island, where I grew up. Through the kitchen window I see a group of people—it looks like a family—hanging around in the front yard. There are four young men, all carrying sawed-off shotguns. Three girls, who look to be in their teens, have their heads covered. Though I know it's a mistake, curiosity gets the better of me. I open the door.

"Can I help you?" I ask, my tone something between an invitation and a threat. No one answers. They stare at me. I understand they want to come inside.

Change du scene. They are inside now, although I have no recollection of admitting them. They mill about our tiny kitchen and living room, so many of them they fill the ground floor. I climb the stairs to the second floor, where my father has put a double bed in the narrow hallway for my two younger brothers, leading to a bedroom with two bunk beds for my older brother and me. I am surprised to encounter one of the uninvited guests standing there, looking around at our sparse furnishings, as if for something to steal.

"All right, you need to leave now," I say to the man.

He doesn't speak. He is a large man, unarmed, and from the way he looks at me I can tell that while he acquiesces in leaving my room, he has no intention of leaving the house.

I am alone now, in my childhood bedroom above the garage where Frank and I slept in beds with thin mattresses amidst the bric-a-brac of our youth. A watercolor Frank did of a four-mast schooner is thumbtacked to the plasterboard wall. Frank inherited some of our mother's artistic talent.

I hear someone climbing the stairs. I leave the bedroom to intercept them and see one of the teenage girls climbing the stairs, head down. I find a block of wood and call out a warning. She lifts her covered head, and I make a threatening motion with the block of wood. Three of the men folk have gathered at the foot of the stairs to watch. The girl hesitates, then keeps coming. I come down two steps, grab her around the waist and start dragging her back down the stairs. The men folk, still speechless, start climbing up to get involved.

My heart sinks. I am a prisoner in my own house.

Beyond belief. Hillary found a way to lose again. Donald Trump has been elected president. Fear stalks the land.

All we can think about now is "Just how bad will it be?" If he comes anything close to doing what he has threatened to do, then we are looking at the end of the American Era. The headline stories in the papers and on CNN are all about Trump's cabinet picks. John Cleese, on Twitter, sums it up best: "It seems Trump is assembling a crew for a pirate ship." Newt Gingrich, for some reason left out of the lineup, risibly urges Trump to "Drain the Swamp", as if he were not one of its principal inhabitants.

Trump has also cast off some of his campaign promises, a month and a half before he takes office. No, he won't jail Hillary. Waterboarding? His pick for the National Security Council, General Kelly, tells him that two beers and a pack of cigarettes works better when getting terrorists to sing. Trump likes this approach: the presidency by sound bite. His coterie of sycophants take note.

I am in London when Mimi has her Memorial Service, so I ask Kate, who is attending, to deliver my remarks for me:

To say that Mimi was the best thing that happened to John, and vice versa, is no exaggeration. In the forty-three years Juanito and I have worked together, it's fair to say that from the moment he and Mimi became a couple, Juanito, always a visionary and Key Man in the crusade to end world poverty, became a thousand times more organized, productive and effective. In Mimi he had the perfect life partner, someone as passionate and dedicated as he was to the mission, but also someone who embodied the famous "life-work" balance many speak of but few actually achieve. Mimi used to say that people warned her that Juanito was the type of person who would always love FINCA more than he would love any woman.

"Of course he loves FINCA more than me," she rejoined. "But FINCA is a worthy competitor for my affections. Better FINCA than something like the pursuit of wealth and money."

But Mimi was wrong. Juanito did love her more than FINCA, and the proof of this is his absolute devotion to her happiness, and the fact that he always put her first when it counted. I have never known a more nurturing couple, one that held together through good times and bad. There were tragedies in both their lives that would have sorely tested the bonds of any couple, but Juanito and Mimi saw it all through, together.

Juanito, I know the sadness you must be feeling now, but take heart from the great group of people, close and far, whose lives you have made infinitely better through your work and your friendship. We will see you through this. And speaking for myself and Lorraine, we are sorry to be across the sea today, but I will join you soon and we will commemorate in proper fashion Mimi's life and times. I'm with you, hermano. Kate, I direct you to give this man a heartfelt hug on my behalf.

MEXICO LINDO Y QUERIDO

2016, the Year of the Reaper, is winding down. I almost forgot about my neighbor, Paulo, who appears now only occasionally in his beloved garden, moving about his trees and shrubs like an incarnate spirit with one eye on the hereafter, his facial features shrunk down to a single expression of anguish, his body thinned out by some terminal malady; I'm guessing cancer. This morning, I notice a Christmas tree tied to the roof of his car in the driveway.

Lorraine tells me something that relieves me greatly: she no longer wants to sell the house and move to either the UK or to Rhode Island. The strain on our budget is great, with three mortgages gnawing at our paychecks, plus the burden of supporting two of our three children. We will manage! Perhaps Trump will cut our taxes!

Meanwhile, at FINCA, we toil away, hoping that 2017 will be the year we get back to profitability. We have less pressure on us since we sold Mexico, which netted us about $20 million in cash. Mercutio, however, emails me that Prince Hal and he spoke over Thanksgiving and Prince Hal wants FINCA to dilute down below 50% ownership in the holding as the *sine qua non* for another capital raise. Sorry, Prince Hal, no can do.

After the Mexico sale, Gonzalo, one of my former CEOs, emails me to tell me that he and some other FINCA Mexico alumni are planning to get together at one of our first village banks in Cuatla, the birthplace of FINCA Mexico in the State of Morelos, about 100 kilometers south of Mexico City. His words sting like a nest of fire ants:

The majority of us feel deceived, indignant and disillusioned at this terrible decision to sell this symbol of success not only in the Mexican market but all of Latin America. We will gather together with the members of the first Village Bank ever formed, Las Orquideas, to inform them that we have come to chop down the tree that used to be FINCA, now that it no longer exists to spread the philosophy of FINCA, but rather to be cut up into firewood and sold, just like any other business.

Whew.

I tap out my lame reply:

Yes, a sad day for me, obviously. So many beautiful memories and friends. But the sad truth is that, due to the hits sustained in Azerbaijan and the rest of Eurasia, we don't have sufficient capital to feed the rest of the network, precipitating these difficult but necessary decisions.

On the positive side, the buyer has sufficient capital to expand the institution, and in this way our work continues, albeit under a different flag. These are the times, my brother. There are great disruptions taking place in the financial sector, and we are not exempt from them. The capital we raised from the sale will allow us to expand in other markets with less competition and more people with no access to financial services.

But, yes, it hurts. Please give my apologies to the ladies of Las Orquidias and reassure them that the financial services will continue, and maybe even in an improved form.

This week we received a note from Juanito, thanking us for our "spot-on description of why Mimi was such an inspiration". He speculates that she "is up in Heaven, remodeling the place with Mother Teresa".

Perhaps, after this year, I will not ruminate so much on death. For now, there are too many reminders of the brevity of life for me to deny that my own demise draws closer, day by day. Should I be spending my pocket-change remaining days differently? I don't really have much choice, considering FINCA's situation. I have to leave both FMH and the foundation on a solid financial footing so they can survive and thrive into the future.

EPIPHANY IN THE
KEY OF GEE

It's Board Hell Week. First is the foundation, to be followed by FMH. I brief the other board members of FINCA International on the financial situation of FMH, which is a pretty dismal picture. Since the high point of our Net Asset Value of $305 million back in 2013, we have dropped $100 million to $205 million in three years. Most of this is due to forex losses from the devastating currency depreciations in Azerbaijan, Mexico and the other oil producing countries, except Ecuador, which is dollarized. Even if oil skyrockets back up to $100 per barrel, this won't help us, as by that time Azerbaijan and Mexico will be gone and will have already monetized their Currency Translation Adjustments (CTAs). Most of this hit has been absorbed by our minority shareholders, because we took them in at a premium of 10% and then, in the second round, 20% over our book value. Ah, those were the days! Everything looked so bright.

The sale of Mexico did little to solve our capital problem; I inform the board that, since the sale of our flagship in Latin America, we have offers to buy almost every other subsidiary in the network. Our shareholders may think we suck, but for the rest of the world, to pick up a FINCA sub is a real prize. The discussion then takes an unexpected turn: Why don't we sell all of Latin America and Eurasia and put the proceeds in our big markets in Nigeria, Congo and Pakistan? After all, there really isn't much left to do in Latin America. The markets are small and saturated. Ecuador is still vulnerable to new shocks, and the loan guarantees we have extended to our creditors hang over us like a forest of Damocles swords.

I am surprised how much appeal this idea holds for me. Even more surprising, I find no dissent, even from my fellow founders, Caesar, Juanito and Mercutio. What is going on here? Can we really be considering selling all those countries? I would have to anticipate a storm of emails from our embittered employees, decrying my having "chopped down the tree of FINCA and sold it for firewood". But to have all that capital to invest in Pakistan and Nigeria! After an initial drop in our client numbers, we might reach millions more in those three large, underserved markets.

I can't believe I am even considering this. My thinking on the "footprint reduction" has evolved, that's for sure.

Lesson Learned Swag Box No. 35: Let It Go
Companies and even whole industries have life cycles, like plants and animals. It is rare for a company to survive and thrive through every phase of the evolution of an industry. FINCA and the other microfinance pioneers thrived through the first decade of the advent of microfinance and did reasonably well during the second decade. In retrospect, I can see that this was largely because FINCA went to new, virgin markets in Africa and Eurasia. As the competition "filled in" behind us, companies that were more innovative or focused on a single country began to overtake us. Our third decade has been a flat-out struggle to survive. My strategy was to go to the last big underserved markets where we would face less competition and have room to grow. But for this to work, we need the resources. With our "Dilution Dilemma" holding us back, perhaps the only alternative we have is to pull capital from our old, saturated markets and invest in the "growing points" in Pakistan, Nigeria, the Congo and Egypt.

The FMH board meeting goes as expected. Our pro bono attorneys from Covington & Burling crush any hopes the minority shareholders have of diluting us below 51% or conceding control over the board. Prince Hal is vexed by this outcome, knowing that it means another year of capital starvation for FMH. He asks that Covington seek an unofficial ruling from the IRS about the language in the charters of KFW and FMO. If their language is similar to FINCA's, this could be grounds for arguing that FINCA's mission isn't at risk, as long as the three entities maintain majority control together. The Covington lawyers are skeptical that this could work.

At the conclusion of the FMH board meeting, after all the resolutions regarding bank accounts and other authorities have been passed, Iago, sitting next to me, says he has one final resolution to put forth. I know what's coming.

"We can put this in more flowery language, but I would like to propose that we recognize the outgoing Co-CEO, Rupert, for his enormous contribution to FMH."

So Iago is my friend again. I thank him for his recognition in the resolution of my "enormous contribution".

GATHERING WOOL

I am on the coast of some unfamiliar nation with Lorraine and my son, John, walking through the ground floor of a beach resort. We pass through a number of large rooms that look more like the waiting rooms in a train station than a beach resort. Each room is crowded with people waiting ... for what? For their rooms to be cleaned and available? It is not clear whether Lorraine, John and I are registered, or where we should go to find out. As yet, we have not found anything that looks like a check-in.

Change du scene. John and I are outside, behind a rolling line of sand dunes, so high they obscure the ocean beyond. Lorraine has disappeared. We mount a high, steep sand dune, and as we reach the summit, the ocean comes into view. It is close to sunset, and the western sky is reddening. Enormous breakers smash onto the sandy beach below. I ask John if he thinks the water is warm enough for swimming. He doesn't answer.

Change du scene. John and I stand atop a high, thin column of firm sand with sides too steep for descending. There is barely room on top for the two of us. The waves are gigantic, even larger than before. Farther out, one rises up like a huge blue-green sea monster, hundreds of feet high. It sucks in the water near the shore, feeding on it to grow in stature.

"It's a tsunami!" John exclaims. "Let's get out of here!"

The descent down the sheer face of the sand dune takes forever. Why has the tsunami not struck? We make it to the base of the pinnacle and hurry towards the entrance to the resort. I keep glancing behind me to make sure John is still following. I go through the same series of waiting rooms in reverse order, still crowded with people, still spare of furniture. I pause and look back. John has disappeared. I wait for him to catch up. I search the faces of the other guests, some of which look familiar, but none recognize me. I realize I can text John and Lorraine and ask them where I can find them. I begin to do so, but before I can, I wake up.

The clock on my nightstand reads 3 a.m.

The year-end compels its requisite amount of wool-gathering. Have we hit bottom? I think so. Enemies still lurk, but for now have gone underground. Prince Hal thinks we can even disband the Restructuring Working Group. Maybe the earthquake in Ecuador and the hurricane in Haiti fulfilled our quota of "Black Swans" for the time being. Ecuador is our best indicator of progress. We are slowly shedding our external debt, replacing it with savings. As a result, we are less held hostage by our creditors. Of the three bidders who vied to buy us a year ago, one has been liquidated (Funal), one is in deep trouble and itself under "intensive supervision", and Alfonso, the handwriting expert-cum-banker, just asked to be my friend on Facebook.

What could go wrong? Our staff has been decimated by the restructuring, and someone, somewhere in the network is surely planning to take advantage of our weakened control environment. I shall warn Rosalind of this.

THE DEVILS WE
KNOW

If it is true you can't accomplish anything important in this world without making enemies, it is also certain that to triumph over them you have to have loyal friends. Mercutio has been one of those for me. Mercutio gave up a big part of his family life in his thirties and forties to throw himself into his workout career. He made big sacrifices, but he also got huge financial rewards, which have left him with a material security rare in this world. Today, retired at fifty, he gives generously of his time to rescue FINCA, a mission his career singularly prepared him for and which he clearly enjoys. Had he not taken that path, then we would not have survived 2016. What could be a better partnership? I spent the past thirty years building out FINCA's footprint on four continents, and now Mercutio is rescuing us from my excesses. We still are on the path, and all will be well. I think about what Juanito used to say in the old days, when everything seemed to go well, and FINCA led a charmed life:

"It's all perfect, bro."

It seems Prince Hal's proposal to disband the Restructuring Group was premature. Our point-man on the Tajikistan transaction, a member of our Capital Markets Group, reports that three of the lenders have totally blown up the deal to roll their loans and give us time to engineer a sale. They have come with new demands that would prohibit us from selling the company or loan portfolio to another party. They want us to deposit $4 million in "hostage money" that they alone control. They are slandering FINCA again, calling us "dishonest" and "untrustworthy".

Well, okay, if that's the way you see it. Here is how we at FINCA see it: We have done our damnedest to get you as much of your money back as possible, and we are doing so *with absolutely no financial benefit to FINCA*. We have lost all our equity in Azerbaijan, we will lose most or all of it in Tajikistan, and we have agreed not to recover any our costs of doing all this *for your benefit.*

Yes, but the benefit to FINCA, we are told, is that we might *not* call all our loans in your other subsidiaries. You might be able to count on us to continue lending to you in the future. And remember: we are all you have, FINCA. We are the only ones in the world who will ever lend to you now.

It appears we will go into 2017 with both Tajikistan and Azerbaijan still as big icebergs gnawing at our hull. What to do? Our outside legal counsel advises us to play the bankruptcy card. Threaten to declare bankruptcy in both countries, which would result in being intervened by the Central Banks, which would mean the lenders don't recover a cent. The risk here is that if we go that route, it will trigger the dreaded Global Standstill. And there is the incalculable blow to our reputation from having a regulated FINCA bank go Chapter 11. The microfinance financial community will go bananas. Mutually assured destruction. You can only do it once.

So we shall, as always, default to bold. Will it work this time? We are counting on the timidity of the species of banker who inhabits these international development agencies. If they were not so risk-averse, they would be in the "real world" of investment banking, on Wall Street, the City in London, or Singapore. We are hoping that when faced with a true disaster that could cost them their jobs, they will flinch.

And, yes, hate us even more than they do now. Above all, they can't stand the fact that this little flea of a non-profit, FINCA, is defying the Mighty International Development Banks. They must walk their corridors, muttering imprecations against us. Stick pins in a Rupert voodoo doll before they turn in at night.

FELIZ NAVIDAD

Mother Nature, with its usual heavy hand, puts a damper on Christmas, which dawns gray, cold and rainy. Enough! There is much to be thankful for. Think of where we were twelve months ago.

And as for me? I survived. In one week, I will pass the reins of FMH over to Rosalind. But I am leaving on my own schedule, the one I agreed with Rosalind, not being forced out by the shareholders. Hooray for me.

So why do I feel so depressed?

I am walking down the street and encounter a man in front of a literary society. I tell him that I am a writer as well, and hand him a copy of *The New Yorker*, referring him to an article I have written and urging him to get in touch with me regarding my next project. I reach for his right hand but he quickly grasps mine in his left. I notice that his right arm is palsied, hanging limp at his side.

Change du scene. I am back at Camp Chewonki, in Wiscasset, Maine, where I spent the summers of my youth. A group of us are hiking out to "The Point", a campsite on the shores of an inlet called Montsweag Creek. I am carrying my guitar. At some point, someone steals it.

Change du scene. I am in a room with some guy, the culprit I assume, and he is offering me various substitutes for my Martin. No, I tell him, I want my Martin back. Give it to me.

I awake, brushing off the remnants of the dream, and rush downstairs to open the case of my Martin.

Whew.

As the reader will have discerned, my nightmares tend to fall into two general categories: Sports-Themed and Precipice-Situated. I have a theory regarding the former. It was my senior year at Brown, and I had exhausted all my ploys to avoid the draft, one of which involved eating four dozen raw eggs the night before my Selective Service physical in order to elevate the albumen level of my urine. I decided I needed a bolder strategy. I resolved to build a record. As a felon.

On a warm evening in the spring of 1971, I drove with some friends down to Newport, Rhode Island, where I deliberately parked in a "Coast Guard Only" space. After a dozen beers at a nearby bar, my friends and I came out to find two Coast Guard MPs standing over my Ford Cortina. I proceeded to argue with them. I accused them of infringing on my human rights. This had the desired effect: they packed us all off to the overnight lockup.

The next morning, after an appearance before a local judge, who was, fortuitously, a Brown Man, we were released on our own recognizance. By now it was noon, and I had a lacrosse game at 3 p.m. It was against Holy Cross, whom we always defeated by double digits. Just in case, as I had not slept in my cool, narrow cell, I popped a pair of greenies to animate myself.

I made it back to Providence just in time. Almost just in time. With five minutes to go before the opening faceoff, I hastily donned my uniform and equipment, grabbed my stick and ran out to take my place with the First Midfield. I was looking forward to stretching my legs after a night in a cramped cell. Coach Stevenson had other ideas.

"Scofield, where have you been? Get off the field. You're sitting this one out."

SELFIE

Default to Bold, *Rupert Scofield's long-anticipated follow-up to his breakout bestseller* The Social Entrepreneur's Handbook, *part tell-all business drama, part nearly extinct genre travelogue, is a harrowing cautionary tale for any entrepreneur contemplating opening up his capital to outside investors. Told with wit, total transparency and, at times, seething rage, Scofield again demonstrates he is the master of the non-boring business book.*

A FAREWELL TO ARMS

In London, my PR firm organizes a breakfast with a dozen journalists, all of whom want to know my opinion of our new president. Trump has shocked the world during his first week in office, his vanity and narcissism on full display as he tries to explain why more people turned out to protest his taking office than to celebrate his inauguration. His Official Liar, Spicer, gives a "briefing" to the press where he reiterates Trump's preposterous, demonstrably false claim to have drawn a bigger inaugural crowd than at the beginning of Obama's first term. He churns out Executive Orders which undo everything Obama accomplished in trade and healthcare. What kind of fool, on his first day, tears up a trade agreement he has never read, let alone analyzed? It reminds me of when Bush, his first week, blew up the nuclear talks in North Korea, assuming Clinton didn't know what he was doing. The result? North Korea will soon have a bomb. Trump is, like Bush and Cheney, a destroyer who exults in bringing down the work of other men his intellectual and moral superior.

For the journalists' edification, and to avoid generating a headline that could cause FINCA and me trouble back home, I suggest that Trump might take a private sector approach to Foreign Assistance in synch with FINCA's strategy of partnering with social enterprises. In my heart, however, I am deeply pessimistic about the Trump presidency and look forward to the coming four years with the same relish a Dark Ages Londoner did the Bubonic Plague.

The next day I fly to Dubai to attend Rosalind's Global Management Meeting. All our CEOs and COOs from our twenty-one subsidiaries have gathered there to talk about our plans for 2017. I am only staying two nights, and have been given just a half hour to talk about the future role of the foundation. While it's great to see all the members of our team in one place, in truth, I feel awkward and somewhat unwelcome. It's Rosalind's show now. While I'm still on the board of the holding company, I no longer have any executive responsibility. People tell me I look younger. Maybe the reduced burden has had a salubrious effect on my health. But it feels strange, and one part of me wants to get out of there as soon as possible.

Mercutio is here, and Iago and Prince Hal as well. Iago and I are friends again; the trials of the past year seem distant and irrelevant now. With less "skin in the game", I can look more objectively at my own performance and legacy. Horatio tells me we have a choice coming up: we can take all the Currency Translation Adjustments (CTAs) from the Azerbaijan debacle in 2016, producing a loss in the $50 million range, or we can push them into 2017, which will mean our third year in a row in the red. The CTAs hide in your balance sheet like time bombs until you undertake a transaction—a sale or a liquidation—at which time they explode in a burst of red ink in what accountants call "Other Comprehensive Income (or losses)". We have several such time bombs in our balance sheet, especially in Azerbaijan and Eurasia, but also in the other countries which have suffered big currency devaluations against the dollar.

I don't have to guess which Horatio prefers. Rosalind has told me his goal is to draw a bright line between the current management of FMH and "The Rupert Era". I am peeved at the way Horatio seems to always withhold the really bad news until the last moment, and then drop something on us that completely changes the financials, and for the worse. When I tell Rosalind and Mercutio about this, they act surprised.

As we near the end of this drama, wherein I have pilloried adversaries and friends alike for their foibles, it would hardly be fair not to own up to my own. Have I been in denial, all these past eighteen months? What would I think of a manager who left his company with a total of $100 million in losses? Surely it can't *all* be due to external shocks?

Let's start with Latin America. How is it possible that in the region I know best, where I cut my teeth, stubbed my toes, choose your metaphor, I could commit my most grievous fuck-ups? My stewardship there was appallingly deficient. Every single Regional Manager was a mistake, including Rocky, whose many talents and vast experience never included the ability to juggle a half dozen countries at the same time. None of the Country CEOs I promoted were up to that challenge either. Lady Macbeth and Iago were right on that one: it was a failure to focus. I was too besotted with my adventures in the new, unexplored parts of the world to pay adequate attention to Latin America. Carlos, one of our board members in Ecuador, issued repeated warnings ("Rupert, I am really worried about Latin America."), all of which went unheeded, and as our competition raised its game, the FINCA subsidiaries in LA remained mired in the past, failing to modernize. Worse, the problem continues to this day. We have good management, finally, in three of the subs, but we are weak in Haiti and Guatemala, and above all we don't have the leadership at the regional level. And I can't make Rosalind see this. There's something about Latin America that blinds people.

But by far my most egregious error was to delegate the stewardship of my relationships with FINCA lenders and share-holders to my Chief Financial Officers. As long as things are going well, this can be the right strategy, allowing you as the CEO to focus on Operations and Strategy. But CFOs, God bless them, are seldom "people people". These key relationships, at the end of the day, are the responsibility of the CEO. That would be me. I did not nurture them. I did not call all my counterparts in my six shareholders once a quarter—admit it, not even once a year!—to let them know what was going well and what not so much. Maybe fifty lenders were too many to call, but I should have called the top ten

By the time things had gone south in such a big way, it was too late to rectify this boo boo. Even my greatest ally, Prince Hal, advised me to step aside and let Rosalind manage these relationships. He was right to do so. It made Rosalind's life a living hell for eighteen months, and arguably made some of the relationships between them and FINCA even more complicated, but by then my "relationship" with those people was beyond salvaging.

Lesson Learned Swag Box No. 36: When the Best Case is Crickets

The time to strengthen relationships with your key stakeholders—be they investors, creditors, or donors—is when things are going well. You may feel it is a waste of time to call them up and say, "Hey, everything is going great! Just thought you would want to know!" But that is the time when you can have a good conversation and suss out any concerns they may have for the longer term, and figure out a way to deal with them. In any case, they will appreciate it.

But don't make the mistake I made and delegate these relationships, and then hope you can revive them after things have gone south. When you call after things have gone south, the best you can hope for on the other end of the line is crickets.

THE SONG IN MY THROAT

The Great War is not over yet, there are still skirmishes here and there, but it is winding down. FINCA is going to survive. Some of our relationships will survive, but others, the trust on both sides irreparably broken, will not. Our many errors capitalized, we will nurture those that remain important to us. When the good times return, we will form new relationships. And who knows? Investors have short memories. And as I know, there are always changes at the top. There could be new personalities who want to rekindle old flames.

FINCA is in a different place now. We are damaged goods. After thirty years with zero defaults, we now wear a big scarlet "D" on our backs. Our creditors have forgiven about $40 million of our loans in Azerbaijan. Horatio, to my surprise and delight, actually sold them on his long-shot strategy. In FMH, we have lost $100 million in capital, about $40 million of it belonging to our minority shareholders. Future investors and creditors alike will approach us with caution.

I feel bad about this. At the same time, as our workout advisors at M&A constantly remind us, our stakeholders would have done exactly as we did, were positions reversed. Think of a financial crisis as the sinking of the *Titanic*, when the only thing you can count on is everyone is going to look after his own survival. The only way FINCA could have made our creditors in Azerbaijan whole would have been to commit financial suicide. And let us not forget that in Azerbaijan we had a very long, profitable run, in which most of our creditors participated. The ones who were in at the beginning did very well, even taking into account the 25% haircut. (In fact, at this writing, the haircut has decreased to 20% and some of our creditors are even asking: "Why doesn't FINCA stay?") If one believes that, in these kinds of very risky markets, not only the rewards but also the losses should be shared, then FINCA has no cause to feel ashamed.

And what of our clients? Who looked after their interests? Sadly, no one. FINCA, to our credit, tried the hardest, but none of our investors nor lenders cared enough about them to try to save the institution so it could keep providing services to our clients. They are now left to fend for themselves, as they did before FINCA arrived. And herein lies the great warning to all social entrepreneurs who take in "social", "impact", or "patient" investors. They will be one or all three as long as the profits are there. When the profits vanish, regardless of the reason, they will shuck their "social" raiment and turn as ruthless as the worst of the wolves of Wall Street. Everyone knows this. It's the dirty secret of our sector.

But wait: there are exceptions, and this is the place to recognize one. Deutsche Bank did a sub debt deal with us seven years ago, a multi-country note, of which one was Azerbaijan. The note almost made it to maturity, but lost 100% of its value in the last year. DB never complained (at least to us); neither did its High Net Worth Investors. The reaction of the latter was: "Well, we had six good years with generous returns, and we almost came out whole. But we knew this could happen; these are risky markets. And we know we did a lot of good for a lot of poor people during the good years. We would probably do it again."

It will take time for us to rebuild our capital. But we have some wildcards up our sleeve, like Pakistan. An IPO there could give us the kind of payday that ACCION achieved with

Compartamos. And those shareholders who "knew when to hold 'em" will share in that wealth event, *Inshallah.*

I wake early. I feel an abiding despair. Signs in storefronts: *Up to 50% Off!* A young couple, kissing at an intersection, unmindful that the light has turned green. An old woman with a small dog, pausing to allow it to urinate on the dead flowers at the base of a leafless tree. Every familiar object seems a reminder that my time here is limited, winding down. *A Wind-Down Agreement.* This is what we are negotiating in Azerbaijan. To paraphrase John Updike, business failure rehearses death. A reminder that everything we do in the short space of our lifetimes will, ultimately, be brought down. Sometimes, though, life is cruel and the "ultimately" comes into play while we are still around to witness it. As helpless bystanders.

Is this the cause of my dark ruminations, so common these days? I think it goes beyond what is happening at FINCA.

I get an idea which I suppose is brilliant. Today, April 2, 2017, one day after April Fools' Day, I just figured it all out. FI will be the risk-taker, FMH the profit-taker. We can bury the hatchet with IFC. We can end the War. Pax Americana.

Lesson Learned Swag Box No. 37: Leave a Clean Campsite

Before I promoted Rosalind to CEO, I changed out my Chief Technology Officer and my Human Resources Director. I knew she didn't want either of them, and I also came to realize that of late I had been spending an inordinate amount of my time fighting their battles for them in a vain attempt to help them regain the credibility they had lost with the rest of the team through a series of setbacks. I wanted to leave Rosalind as clear a field as possible for her to make her own hires into these key positions.

Your direct reports in your top staff should be people who take monkeys off your back, not folks who put our

screeching little primate cousins on, their spindly, hairy little arms around our necks, choking us. If you find yourself devoting too much time to helping them resolve their problems so they can do their job, then you have the wrong person in that position. They should only be coming to you when there is an intractable problem that they can't resolve using their own ingenuity and powers of persuasion. Yes, it may take considerable effort and time to find a suitable replacement. And there is the risk, of course, of making another mistake. You have to take that chance. So get on with it.

This life has gone too fast. I look back with disbelief on all that has transpired, the victories and the defeats, the satisfactions and the disappointments, the allies and the enemies. At times I reflect upon my time being bored to death in my high-school class room, those days when life moved at the pace of a tortoise, when my future was no more clear than a pitcher of ink. I marvel at the path I took, and how much of it relied upon pure fate versus calculation. At the risk of cliché, I really can't improve upon that Frank Sinatra song "My Way". To think, we did all that.

It's not over yet! There are adventures still to come, as we try to find the next winning business model, and help millions more people to a better life, even as the madness around us— civil wars, terrorists, selfish, incompetent leaders—continues. Alongside the madness and the countless reasons for despair and to lose hope, there are monumental positive changes taking place in this world that promise a better future for all of mankind. The science and the tools are all there. The will and the intelligence to deploy them is all we lack. And I am going to do my part, for as long as I am able.

I may as well admit it. I love this job.

EPILOGUE

I thought about starting to write again today. Nine months have passed since I handed over the reins of FMH to Rosalind. On August 2, 1917, while on a mission to Egypt, I fell victim to a life-altering health event that left me physically and psychologically damaged. One of the worst side effects of this malady is that for an indefinite period the victim succumbs to a severe depression in which he is unable to do any of the things that he loves, that used to sustain him. One of these, for me, has always been writing.

Another has been FINCA, of course. I cannot say the transition, even before my incident, has been easy. I have the much-reduced remit of running the foundation, and our new FINCA Plus initiative, challenging enough as any startup, but not the same. And it's not that I want my old job back. I did the right thing for FINCA, passing the baton. And I kept my promise to Roz, turning over the helm to her. She's uniquely equipped to be my successor, having both the brainpower for the strategy and the heart for the mission. And the ordeal of the past two years has toughened her up, which will undoubtedly come in handy for the trials ahead.

Still, I don't know how else to say it. I just miss it.

Today, a few weeks later, I am actually taking up my figurative pen again. I think I can at last relate the story of what befell me, three months ago, in the departure lounge of the Cairo airport, hoping to catch a plane to Dubai and then on to Nairobi.

The best way to describe a stroke is that you feel as though you are Superman and someone entered the room with a rock of Kryptonite. You suddenly lose all your powers: to stand, to talk, to walk—everything. I don't use the Man of Steel metaphor lightly. Up until that day I had felt invulnerable to the major contretemps of life, protected, perhaps, by a supernatural power, with the caveat that this would be for as long as I stayed true to my values—stayed on the path, as it were.

This is what happened, near as I can make out:

We had gone to the airport early, my Lebanese colleague, Hassan, and I, hoping to avoid the worst of the Cairo traffic, responsible for many a missed flight. As it turned out, we were far too early, and found ourselves in the antechamber, within the airport and on the other side of the first security barrier. This configuration is common in developing country airports, which have suffered many attacks at the unguarded entrances to airports. They will remain unattended in so-called developed countries until the terrorists start blowing up the passengers *before* they enter the airport to check in. The attack on the Belgian airport was the first of these and no doubt will turn out to have been the precursor to many more.

We arrived two hours before the Emirates check-in desk opened, and were left to wait in a kind purgatory between the inner and outer security checkpoints, where neither food nor beverages were available. I was feeling out of sorts, having spent a week battling an intestinal affliction since my visit to Pakistan a week earlier. I had drunk some water earlier in the day, and was taking Cipro, which no doctor recommends but which kills anything living in your GI tract, malign or benign.

I remember I called my wife, Lorraine, to inform her of my situation. I was feeling very weak, which I attributed to having eaten nothing since breakfast, some eight hours earlier. A fellow traveler took pity on me and offered some of his dates. A fracas broke out at the security checkpoint when one of the guards tried to confiscate a female traveler's beaker of perfume.

She lost the altercation and the goods went into the security guards' inventory. I still felt weak, but able enough to finally check in for my flight, and even make it through immigration.

But at the inner security checkpoint, just before the boarding gates, my strength failed me. Although I didn't faint, I couldn't get my carry on through the X-ray machine, and I had to sit down after passing through the metal detector. There I sat, for twenty minutes or so, until I felt well enough to accompany a helpful female traveler to the Emirates lounge.

Once inside the lounge, my erratic behavior must have drawn the attention of the flight attendants, who summoned the Airport Doctor. Unfortunately for me, the AD had apparently never encountered nor been trained to recognize symptoms such as I exhibited—disorientation, difficulty standing and holding things. Therewith began a kind of crowd-sourced medical consultation involving a few doctors also traveling on Emirates, but mostly well-meaning passengers with no medical experience who were concerned but, like the Airport Doctor, clueless as to what had befallen me.

Finally, after perhaps two hours in the lounge, the AD came to me to deliver the verdict: the consensus of the ad hoc consultative group was that I should not fly. I was to go instead to a hospital, via an ambulance that was already being dispatched.

A wheelchair arrived, my luggage was retrieved, and I was taken outside. Here, a huge altercation erupted, which I could not follow since it was all in Arabic. What I eventually surmised, in hindsight, is that the members of the consultative group disagreed as to which hospital should receive me, and how I should get there.

Also with the benefit of hindsight, I came to understand that during this waiting period, and additional time spent at the hospital, valuable hours were lost. At the hospital, a byzantine, gray, gloomy-looking facility, my admittance was delayed by efforts by the ambulance staff to get me to pay for it (as if it were a taxi), which I could not, as I had virtually no cash on me. The driver contented himself with taking what I had in my wallet, a U.S. twenty and a few Swiss banknotes from an earlier stop on my trip.

Thereafter, I was deposited in the Intensive Care Unit, and left there for at least two hours. Finally, a full six hours after my incident first struck, I was administered a blood thinner to unblock the veins causing the obstruction in my brain. I learned, subsequently, that what I had suffered was known as a Transient Ischemic Attack (TIA) or mini-stroke, which causes a temporary deprivation of oxygen to the brain. If treated opportunely (within four hours), it goes away within a day. This did not happen in my case. Valuable time was lost, and my TIA turned into a regular stroke. I awoke the following morning with my left arm and leg paralyzed.

I spent the next five days in the Cairo hospital, while a procession of doctors visited me briefly, each to give his or her diagnosis as to what had befallen me, and, more important, how I would recover and how long this would take. I was subjected to tests of all kinds during this period, on equipment that looked to be taken from a *Flash Gordon* movie set. Most annoying to me was the behavior of the orderlies assigned to me. One, in particular, was a young man who periodically would come to my bedside, gaze searchingly into my face and ask in English: "Why aren't you smiling? Why aren't you laughing?" I didn't state the obvious: that, to me, there was nothing remotely risible about my situation. He persisted, day after day, with these interrogations, as if it were my obligation to keep him entertained.

The nights were equally unpleasant. During these long sleepless intervals, new patients would be wheeled in and out, many of them victims of traffic accidents, who lay screaming on their cots, and—for all I knew—bleeding to death.

Mercifully, my daughter Michelle's boyfriend, Simeon, who was a medical student in his final year, arrived one day to announce he was there to bust me out and take me to London, where a renowned neurologist, the father of his roommate at Cambridge, had agreed to take my case. Thus was I rescued.

One of the good things about this whole horrible ideal was the support I got from Lorraine and my children. Lorraine was my advocate across the board, fighting for me with the medical insurance companies (they wanted to leave me in Cairo, because the healthcare was cheap) and subordinating everything in her life to the imperatives of my recovery program. Julie flew all the way from Seattle to "save Grandpa" (a quote from my granddaughter, Lucy). I also had stern words from my son, John, who reminded me of all the important things I was working on, and above all the people at FINCA who looked to me for leadership and were counting on me.

Of the difficult things I have done in my life, perhaps the hardest was holding a staff retreat in September, less than two months after my Kryptonite Encounter. I dreaded this appearance, fearful that my lingering difficulties with walking and writing would be obvious. But Julie (who works part-time for FINCA) assured me that I did fine, and few people noticed. I can admit now that it required a huge effort. While I knew that having FINCA to keep me occupied was an essential part of my rehabilitation, and kept me from spending too much time fretting about the slow pace of my recovery (I was actually told by everyone that I "looked great"), the pace still seemed glacial. If there was progress it was in the way the quotidian matters of FINCA and my personal life began to crowd out my dark obsession with larger concerns surrounding my health. My biggest concern, above all, was whether I remained vulnerable to a second stroke.

Central to this concern (still unanswered) was the question: Why did I have a stroke in the first place? My GP assured me that I had none of the typical risk factors, namely high blood pressure or diabetes. Nor did I smoke, save for the occasional Cuban. The CAT Scans and cardio exams from Cairo showed nothing abnormal, nor did the much more extensive MRA from the London hospital. We were left, then, with theories from the neurologists. My London neurologist concluded it was probably congenital, owing to narrow veins in my brain. The first doctor I saw in Washington disagreed, and pointed to a series of minute spots in the MRA which he said could indicate Lyme's Disease, which is associated with strokes. My current neurologist is going to test me for sleep apnea, which has also been identified both as a causal factor and sometimes a consequence.

Great. And if this test leads nowhere, we are going to try hooking me up to electrodes for four weeks searching for a heart murmur.

I find myself, in other words, still in *terra incognita*, a bad place to be when it comes to serious medical conditions.

Many decades ago, I once told a girlfriend I wanted to turn my life into a novel. *"Esto es la cosa más linda que tu has dicho,"* she told me, which means: "This is the most beautiful thing you've ever said." And in a way I had. Except now the end of the novel wasn't turning out the way it was supposed to. And it was no longer in Technicolor, but in grainy black and white. As one ages, life redeems the blessings it once bestowed, one by one. You then have a choice: spend the balance of your days lamenting what you've lost and complaining, making yourself and those around you miserable, or reflecting on all that has gone right with your world. That requires more effort than you ever imagined it would. But it's still the right choice.

This whole ordeal is possibly forcing a decision I have been putting off: Is it time to change my lifestyle? Is it time to slow down, and to rejigger my priorities? Will writing continue to be a big part of my life, or any? Above all, will the things I relied on to stay sane and happy in the past have to change now? And if so, how? Maybe it's time to make a list:

Less:
Hectic, crammed schedule; particularly travel.
Always working on every weekend.

More/Different:

Travel for business only when absolutely necessary—delegate it when possible.

No more "chain trips" involving three or more countries.

More time for friends and family.

I am recently returned from Los Angeles—a kind of trial trip, as it were—to deliver the keynote address at a Conference on Blockchain and Cryptocurrencies, a subject I know next to nothing about. Actually, my London PR firm set it up, thinking it might be interesting to the organizers to have a Fossil from Finance's Past give some context about what it was like to disrupt the financial industry twenty years ago with microfinance. I guess it worked, as my remarks were very well-received, particularly by the younger attendees.

There is evidence that I might have started to keep the Black Dog at bay again. The things that used to give me pleasure—writing, reading, music—have once again begun to acquire their tang. Never again will I take these—least of all my health—for granted.

In the meantime, I soldier on through my job at FINCA. Surely the reader has grasped the irony newly arisen in the title of this book, and having seen the more or less felicitous outcome for FINCA, whose "turnaround" is, if not complete, at least at the "beginning of the beginning" stage. Will the author's turnaround follow a similar course? Stay tuned.

What I lost that day was more than the usual casualties to depression: sleep, etc. Most of us don't give much thought to our mortality. It's the real life equivalent to "suspending disbelief" temporarily to better enjoy a work of fiction. I can't live in denial anymore. I shall not live forever in my current form. I know it sounds absurd, but up to this point I actually wondered if I could. At least in one sense, I have lost the ability to rely on all the wonderful distractions our beautiful world provides—love, nature, etc.—and must now face the facts: it's coming for me, just as it came for all those before me. I find new sympathy for my departed friends. I dwell on all they have missed since they passed on.

Enough about me. FINCA is doing well. FMH made $10 million in 2017, Roz's first year flying solo. Bravo! FINCA Plus is finding its feet more every day. There is still much to prove, but I know we have the team to do it.

EPILOGUE II
One Year Out

It is just a few days from the first (I hope there will be at least twenty-five more to celebrate) anniversary of my Cairo stroke. Am I totally back? Close to it. The vestiges that remain are fine motor skill gaps, like my still error-prone keystrokes when I type too fast or miss pick notes on my guitar on songs I used to play fluidly. It may come back eventually with more practice. Or it may not.

My mental acuity is there, but it never really changed—just following the well-worn path towards the Happy Hunting Ground, blazed by progressively longer data retrieval times, W. Bush-like malapropisms and amusing word substitutions.

I think about that dream I had where I reached for the withered hand of the writer and found it unresponsive—was this some kind of precognitive event, my body trying to warn me it was about to go haywire? And what about that Global Transient Amnesia episode where my memory went on Leave-Without-Pay for four hours? Am I supposed to believe there was no connection? In any case, I will pay more attention if something like those incidents reoccurs.

I even wonder if what befell me in Cairo was barter for Fordy's miraculous and medically improbable recovery? When we went for his latest checkup, in January of 2018, Dr. Brenstein informed us that the Angiogram was clean: no sign of the swollen Vein of Galen. It had fixed itself. If it were some kind of deal I subconsciously made with the Devil, I am happy to have paid the price.

Caesar was likewise blessed on the health front. His wife has recovered fully from what turned out to be a benign brain tumor.

Meanwhile, FINCA chugs on, shoulder to the mountain. Some of our subsidiaries are still struggling, but Tajikistan and even Azerbaijan, against all odds, have survived. Some of the lenders have even agreed to support them again. Regarding FINCA Plus, our new business model is beginning to prove out. It's not as simple as microfinance, involving as it does sectors that are new to us—energy, water and sanitation, education and agriculture—but these are vital to our customers so we must master them. At least to the extent we can recognize companies that have winning ideas and the teams to scale them up. We will leverage our strengths in these new spaces: the ability to design appropriate credit products, experience and knowledge of these challenging markets, and a network of banks with millions of customers. I feel it all coming together again. We are starting the journey anew. I will be here at the beginning. It will go on without me. That's an eerie thought. But one I find less threatening. I have a good feeling.

In any case, come what may, the winning strategy is clear: Default to Bold.

July 28, 2018
Lahore, Pakistan

Made in the USA
Middletown, DE
11 January 2019